Language Lessons for a Living Education

MASTER BOOKS
— CURRICULUM —

Author: Kristen Pratt

Master Books Creative Team:

Editor: Laura Welch

Design: Jennifer Bauer

Cover Design: Diana Bogardus

Copy Editors:
Judy Lewis
Willow Meek

Curriculum Review:
Kristen Pratt
Laura Welch
Diana Bogardus

First printing: February 2019
Fifth printing: March 2022

Master Books®, P.O. Box 726, Green Forest, AR 72638

Master Books® is a division of the New Leaf Publishing Group, Inc.

ISBN: 978-1-68344-138-0

ISBN: 978-1-61458-679-1 (digital)

Unless otherwise noted, Scripture quotations are taken from the New American Standard Bible® (NASB). Copyright © 1960, 1962, 1963, 1968, 1971, 1972, 1973, 1975, 1977, 1995 by The Lockman Foundation. Used by permission. www.Lockman.org.

Printed in the United States of America

Please visit our website for other great titles:
www.masterbooks.com

About the Author:

Kristen Pratt works as an author and Curriculum Editor for Master Books, where she has been writing curriculum and consulting for the past eight years. She has been homeschooling her nine children for over twenty years, having graduated five so far from high school. She has helped thousands of homeschool families navigate curriculum choices through her own curriculum business and now through the Master Books® communities online and via the app.

All images are from shutterstock.com or istockphotos.com except page 65 public domain; and pages 29, 111, 149, 195, 233, 283, and 321 from Superstock.com

Scope and Sequence

Using This Course

Features: The suggested weekly schedule enclosed has easy-to-manage lessons that guide the reading, worksheets, and all assessments. The pages of this guide are perforated and three-hole punched so materials are easy to tear out, hand out, grade, and store. Teachers are encouraged to adjust the schedule and materials needed in order to best work within their unique educational program.

From root words to analogies: Go in-depth with the course into the eight parts of speech, different types of verbs and verb agreement, plural pronouns, comparisons, prefixes, suffixes, prepositions, contractions, synonyms, antonyms, root words to help determine the meaning of new words, homophones, homonyms, silent letters, writing strong and descriptive paragraphs, learning the parts of a story, double consonant words, letter writing, quotation marks and more!

🕐	Approximately 20 to 30 minutes per lesson, five days a week
🔑	Includes answer keys for worksheets
✏️	Worksheets
📄	Reviews are included to help reinforce learning and provide assessment opportunities
🔄	Designed for grade 4 in a one-year course

Course Objectives: Students completing this course will:

- Master state of being verbs, action verbs, and possessive nouns
- Review sentences, singular and plural nouns, adjectives and adverbs
- Identify abbreviations, proper use of punctuation marks, spelling, root words, compound words, and suffixes
- Create their own dictionary with words learned through the course
- Learn to create good paragraphs based on structure and comprehension
- Develop skills in using the dictionary and a thesaurus for spelling and vocabulary-building
- Explore the Scripture, parts of letter writing, copywork, and more!

Course Description

Language Lessons for a Living Education 4 is a Charlotte Mason–flavored approach to elementary language arts. Enjoy an engaging and effective language arts program for your elementary student. Students will move beyond pages of text and memorization to make real-world connections. This exciting new series will help guide your young learner toward mastery of reading, grammar, and vocabulary, as well as the mechanics of communication and writing. Utilizing observation and reading comprehension through poems, stories, and real books as the foundation, your student will continue to build paragraph writing skills.

The course is a story-based approach, using Charlotte Mason ideas for the modern homeschool student with character-building themes. Each quarter has five stories, two picture studies (one of which is biblically-based), and two poems (one of which is a psalm). Using the spelling words and the Dictionary Worksheets, the student will create his or her very own dictionary week by week through the material. This course incorporates picture study, memorization, grammar and punctuation, spelling and vocabulary, observation, and application through creating their own stories through pictures, sentences, paragraphs, poems, psalms, and letters. This course also develops reading skills and gently develops narration skills. Writing stamina is built up gradually. By the end of the course, students should be able to comfortably write a four to five sentence paragraph.

Required Course Materials: This course has an integrated reading component that uses *101 Favorite Stories from the Bible*, also available from Master Books.

A Note from the Author

This course was written with inspiration from classic educators like Charlotte Mason and Emma Serl. It was also inspired by homeschool educators like David Marks, Angela O'Dell, Katherine (Loop) Hannon, and my colleagues, Craig Froman and Laura Welch. If you could put these people in a room, you would find they all have different thoughts on how to educate a child, yet they have all taught me something that has gone into this series. I have taken the effective principles from long ago and updated them for a modern world with the hope of inspiring a new generation to communicate their faith, and the gospel, to their generation.

A special thanks goes to Becki Dudley who wrote most of the stories in this level. Thank you to Craig Froman who created the Create Your Own Dictionary concept. Also, thank you to Diana Bogardus for creating the cover, which set the tone and beautiful feel of this course. Thank you to Jennifer Bauer for the hours of design work to marry function with beauty. Thank you to Laura Welch and the proofers for their insight and wisdom.

I am indebted to the Moms of Masterbooks who give us valuable feedback on how to improve our curriculum to meet their needs. We do this for them and their children. It is our goal to come alongside them and provide the tools so they can bring up a godly generation, known by the Lord. When the days feel long, I think of the impact our work is having on homeschooled children, and my strength is renewed. Thank you for allowing us to partner with you in the education of your children.

Of course, my children have taught me for many years principles of education that have surprised and inspired me. I have often marveled that nine children can grow up in the same home and be so different from each other. We truly are wonderfully and fearfully made. I have learned from them that curriculum needs to be flexible to meet the needs of the unique individuals God has entrusted to our care.

May God bless and keep you and give you wisdom and strength as you homeschool your children in the nurture and admonition of the Lord.

Blessings,

Kristen Pratt

About This Course

Children enjoy patterns. They like to have rhythms in life that they can count on. This course is set up in a pattern that students and teachers alike can rely on.

The first day of the weekly schedule is a special feature. Every other week starts with a short story. The weeks in between alternate between picture studies and reading poetry or a psalm. (Each quarter follows this pattern.) A light lesson follows.

The second and third days of the week cover writing topics such as grammar and punctuation. They are the tools put into the hands of the student to develop his or her writing skills.

The fourth day of the week, students read from *101 Favorite Stories from the Bible* by Ura Miller, published by Master Books. These stories may be read out loud by the teacher, student, or both. We encourage students to read as much as possible to strengthen their skills and stamina. There are three narration prompts following each reading. Next, the student will write out a Scripture verse for copy work. The student and teacher should memorize this Scripture verse together. Each story has a beautiful illustration that the student will sketch.

The fifth day is when the student focuses on spelling and vocabulary, building a dictionary of words he or she can use in their writing.

There are patterns within the lessons themselves. Students are given a variety of activities that repeat themselves every so often. This creates familiarity without overdoing repetition.

Students' abilities and stamina can vary widely. While we have provided a Daily Schedule, feel free to adjust the pace according to the needs of your student. We have also given varied types of material in the back of the book to aid in the extra practice of key concepts.

There is review built into the course. You will find some topics repeated regularly. Others are repeated in the last quarter when the student will review most of the material he or she has learned. This is vital at this level since students are still strengthening their writing skills and understanding of grammar. It is the perfect opportunity to shore up any areas the student needs to work on.

We hope you enjoy using this course with your student. It is designed to foster a partnership between student and teacher, with the student gradually taking a lead role. Allowing the student's growing abilities, stamina, and interests to set the pace will allow the student's confidence to strengthen. This confidence is the key that will help unlock communication success.

Stories, Poems, Psalms

The stories, poems, and psalms were designed for the teacher and student to read together. This gives reading practice and experience within the context of a short story or passage. This method fosters a partnership between the teacher and the student. It allows the teacher to see where the student excels and needs some extra instructions. It also gives the student a safe place to practice his or her developing reading skills.

The student should read as much of the story, poem, or psalm as possible. The teacher should help the student sound out difficult words and gently take over the reading if the student tires or is struggling. The goal is to build reading skills and stamina through practice. Care should be taken to stay light-hearted and encouraging with a student that is still working to master reading.

If a student is struggling to read, sometimes his or her short-term memory needs to be developed. Reading is memory intensive. You can work on increasing short-term memory through memory games. You will find some in the back of the book.

The NASB is used for the psalms and all Scripture passages (unless otherwise noted) in this book, but you may use the version you prefer.

Independent Reading

Work with the student to pick a book for the student to read independently throughout each week. Care should be taken to select a book within the student's reading ability.

Depending on the reading ability of the student, the book may be read orally, with the help of the teacher. Students may also choose to read the book independently, asking for help only when they come to a word they cannot read or do not understand.

You will find in the back of this book suggestions and a place to record the books the student has read or plans to read.

Oral Narration

Oral narration (or telling back) helps a student develop listening skills and reading comprehension. These questions will help a student connect with the story and improve basic narration skills.

Oral narration is a skill that needs to be developed. Oral narration teaches the student to pay attention to the story and to think about what is happening. It fosters memory recall, which helps develop reading skills. The questions are meant to gently lead a student to the goal of being able to tell back a story on his or her own, with no prompts. Students will vary greatly in their ability to narrate back to the teacher a whole story. We suggest a slow approach, test the student now and then to see if he or she can do it without the prompts.

Memorization

Throughout the course, there are opportunities to memorize short passages of Scripture, poems, etc. The teacher should participate with the student and memorize them too. Students this age are naturally good at memorizing, but they may need some encouragement. Modeling and working together is the best way to encourage this skill.

The student will be memorizing the names of the books of the Bible as well as the genres. Two weeks are given to learn most sets of books. The teacher should memorize the books with the student. The class in the story earns a prize once they have recited all of the books and a bonus for the genres. It would be fun and rewarding (but optional) for you to provide a small prize for your student after he or she has memorized all the books and a bonus prize for the genres.

Writing a Paragraph

The student will be introduced to writing a paragraph. Each time he or she is asked to write a paragraph, a checklist to remind them of the structure of a paragraph is provided. We have also provided a checklist in the back of the book. The student is given a chance to write a paragraph with a variety of prompts to appeal to many types of students. For example, he or she is asked to write about things he or she likes and are personal to him or her, but sometimes the prompt is a picture.

Students may struggle to write a cohesive paragraph, but they will improve with practice. It is good to remind students about using proper punctuation. If they make a mistake, have them correct it but encourage them with what a great job they did. There are different schools of thought regarding whether to correct spelling mistakes. Some believe the student should fix all mistakes to avoid having the wrong spelling imprinted in his or her mind. Others do not want to discourage the student's writing by having him or her fix spelling mistakes. Students vary widely in their ability and personality. I would encourage approaching it on a case by case basis. You know your student best!

If the student struggles to write a paragraph, you can shorten the assignment to the topic sentence, detail sentence, and a closing sentence. If the struggle is stamina, you may write part of the paragraph for the student. You may also want to have the struggling student organize his or her thoughts by reciting to you what he or she wants to say before starting to write. You can also encourage the student by asking questions to lead him or her through the process. For example, you could say, "Okay, you have a great topic sentence about your cat. What are some things you want to tell about your cat?"

The goal is for the student to improve over the school year, regardless of his or her ability level. Even writers who are slower to learn this skill can learn to love writing through lots of gentle encouragement.

Picture Sketching

Sketching develops hand-eye coordination, observation skills, and overall drawing abilities. Each Bible story has a beautiful image for the student to copy. Some students will be very detailed in their sketches while other students will draw the bare minimum. We encourage teachers to allow students to start where their abilities are. Progress is the goal, not perfection. We want students to enjoy the process. If drawing is difficult for the student, we recommend picking out one element of the picture for the student to draw. The student may want to use colored pencils to bring his or her sketches to life. Be sure to lavish the student's attempts with praise and encouragement.

Spelling and Vocabulary

There are various types of activities to foster experience with words. The student should study how to spell the words and use them as often as possible. Some teachers will have the student start working with the words at the beginning of the week, with mastery expected by the end of the week. Others prefer to give them out at the end of the week and have the student work on them the following week. Some students only work on spelling the day it is assigned in the schedule. There is no right or wrong way to do it. Use the approach that best meets the needs of your students.

Some students will struggle more than others with spelling. We have provided resources in the back of the book that include:

- a list of the spelling words organized by lesson for testing, practice, and Create Your Own Dictionary
- a place to keep a list of words to work on
- extra spelling activities and games
- word shape worksheets for all of the spelling words are available as a free download at masterbooks.com/classroom-aids

Please note: Pronunciations can vary by region. Students are asked to sort spelling words by their vowel sounds in some lessons. Please adjust the assignments and lessons according to the pronunciation used by your family.

Create Your Own Dictionary!

Students will use the spelling words and the dictionary worksheets to create their very own dictionary.

The teacher will need to make copies of the Create Your Own Dictionary sheets in the back of the book as needed. They are also available for download on our website. If the student struggles

to add all of the words to the dictionary, the teacher may allow the student to pick fewer words. Let the student's ability and stamina be the guide.

The student will write out the word and then give a simple definition. He or she may even want to draw a picture.

This is a good opportunity to introduce a children's dictionary to the student. The teacher should demonstrate how to look up words in a dictionary and use it to complete the definitions. The student may use one word or simpler definitions rather than copy directly from the dictionary.

Students are encouraged to remove the dictionary pages and continue to add words to it long after they have finished the course. The teacher may offer blank Create Your Own Dictionary pages for this purpose.

Handwriting

While this is not a formal handwriting course, each time a student writes, it is an opportunity to practice handwriting. It is good to remind students to write neatly, using his or her best penmanship. Copy work at the back of the book may be used for more handwriting practice. We also suggest using Scripture as copy work for handwriting practice.

For Fun!

"Just 4 Fun" activities provide extra thinking and problem solving practice. They are meant to be fun. If a student has difficulty solving an activity, offer hints and encouragement. If the student is unable to find the solution, walk him or her through the process of how to solve the problem. Be sure to provide the answer.

Review

The fourth quarter reviews many of the lessons the student has learned in the first three quarters. This is crucial for students to master the material. The lesson length is longer since the student is familiar with the material. If the student does not have the stamina to complete the longer lessons, there are several options. The teacher may read the work to the student, letting the student do the written portion. The teacher may allow the student to complete some of the problems orally. The teacher may also spread the work over several days, as needed.

Teacher Aids

In the back of the book, you will find a section of Teacher Aids. These aids include assessments, extra practice pages, study sheets, fun games, and more. We encourage you to look through the tools provided to use with your students. They provide opportunities for enrichment and fun as your student learns how to communicate more effectively.

Assessments

Two types of assessments are provided in the Teacher Aids section in the back of the book.

We have provided Quarterly Reviews within the curriculum at the end of each quarter. Each quarter has two Reviews covering punctuation, grammar, and writing. There is also a spelling Review. The Reviews provided each quarter may be used as quizzes or tests for grading purposes. The student may be given access to the study sheets in the back of the book when completing the Reviews.

We have also provided an Assessment form in the back of the book that may be used for grading purposes. It tracks mastery of concepts taught throughout the course.

First Semester Suggested Daily Schedule

Date	Day	Assignment	Due Date	✓	Grade
		First Semester-First Quarter			
Week 1	Day 1	Read Story • Page 21 Complete Lesson 1 Exercise 1 • Page 22			
	Day 2	Complete Lesson 1 Exercise 2 • Page 23			
	Day 3	Complete Lesson 1 Exercise 3 • Page 24-25			
	Day 4	Complete Lesson 1 Exercise 4 • Page 26			
	Day 5	Complete Lesson 1 Exercise 5 • Pages 27-28			
Week 2	Day 6	Picture Study • Page 29 Complete Lesson 2 Exercise 1 • Page 30			
	Day 7	Complete Lesson 2 Exercise 2 • Page 31			
	Day 8	Complete Lesson 2 Exercise 3 • Pages 32-33			
	Day 9	Complete Lesson 2 Exercise 4 • Page 34			
	Day 10	Complete Lesson 2 Exercise 5 • Pages 35-36			
Week 3	Day 11	Read Story • Page 37 Complete Lesson 3 Exercise 1 • Page 38			
	Day 12	Complete Lesson 3 Exercise 2 • Pages 39-40			
	Day 13	Complete Lesson 3 Exercise 3 • Pages 41-43			
	Day 14	Complete Lesson 3 Exercise 4 • Page 44			
	Day 15	Complete Lesson 3 Exercise 5 • Pages 45-46			
Week 4	Day 16	Read Poem • Page 47 Complete Lesson 4 Exercise 1 • Page 48			
	Day 17	Complete Lesson 4 Exercise 2 • Pages 49-50			
	Day 18	Complete Lesson 4 Exercise 3 • Pages 51-53			
	Day 19	Complete Lesson 4 Exercise 4 • Page 54			
	Day 20	Complete Lesson 4 Exercise 5 • Pages 55-56			
Week 5	Day 21	Read Story • Page 57 Complete Lesson 5 Exercise 1 • Page 58			
	Day 22	Complete Lesson 5 Exercise 2 • Pages 59-60			
	Day 23	Complete Lesson 5 Exercise 3 • Page 61			
	Day 24	Complete Lesson 5 Exercise 4 • Page 62			
	Day 25	Complete Lesson 5 Exercise 5 • Pages 63-64			
Week 6	Day 26	Picture Study • Page 65 Complete Lesson 6 Exercise 1 • Page 66			
	Day 27	Complete Lesson 6 Exercise 2 • Pages 67-68			
	Day 28	Complete Lesson 6 Exercise 3 • Page 69			
	Day 29	Complete Lesson 6 Exercise 4 • Page 70			
	Day 30	Complete Lesson 6 Exercise 5 • Pages 71-72			

Date	Day	Assignment	Due Date	✓	Grade
Week 7	Day 31	Read Story • Page 73 Complete Lesson 7 Exercise 1 • Page 74			
	Day 32	Complete Lesson 7 Exercise 2 • Pages 75-76			
	Day 33	Complete Lesson 7 Exercise 3 • Page 77			
	Day 34	Complete Lesson 7 Exercise 4 • Page 78			
	Day 35	Complete Lesson 7 Exercise 5 • Pages 79-80			
Week 8	Day 36	Read Psalm 96 • Page 81 Complete Lesson 8 Exercise 1 • Page 82			
	Day 37	Complete Lesson 8 Exercise 2 • Pages 83-84			
	Day 38	Complete Lesson 8 Exercise 3 • Pages 85-87			
	Day 39	Complete Lesson 8 Exercise 4 • Page 88			
	Day 40	Complete Lesson 8 Exercise 5 • Pages 89-90			
Week 9	Day 41	Read Story • Page 91 Complete Lesson 9 Exercise 1 • Page 92			
	Day 42	Do Lesson 9 Exercise 2 **(Quarter 1 Review)** • Pages 93-95			
	Day 43	Do Lesson 9 Exercise 3 **(Quarter 1 Review)** • Pages 96-98			
	Day 44	Complete Lesson 9 Exercise 4 • Page 99			
	Day 45	Complete Lesson 9 Exercise 5 • Page 100			
First Semester-Second Quarter					
Week 1	Day 46	Read Story • Page 101 Complete Lesson 10 Exercise 1 • Page 102			
	Day 47	Complete Lesson 10 Exercise 2 • Pages 103-104			
	Day 48	Complete Lesson 10 Exercise 3 • Pages 105-107			
	Day 49	Complete Lesson 10 Exercise 4 • Page 108			
	Day 50	Complete Lesson 10 Exercise 5 • Pages 109-110			
Week 2	Day 51	Picture Study • Page 111 Complete Lesson 11 Exercise 1 • Page 112			
	Day 52	Complete Lesson 11 Exercise 2 • Pages 113-114			
	Day 53	Complete Lesson 11 Exercise 3 • Page 115			
	Day 54	Complete Lesson 11 Exercise 4 • Page 116			
	Day 55	Complete Lesson 11 Exercise 5 • Pages 117-118			
Week 3	Day 56	Read Story • Page 119 Complete Lesson 12 Exercise 1 • Page 120			
	Day 57	Complete Lesson 12 Exercise 2 • Pages 121-122			
	Day 58	Complete Lesson 12 Exercise 3 • Pages 123-125			
	Day 59	Complete Lesson 12 Exercise 4 • Page 126			
	Day 60	Complete Lesson 12 Exercise 5 • Pages 127-128			
Week 4	Day 61	Read Poem • Page 129 Complete Lesson 13 Exercise 1 • Page 130			
	Day 62	Complete Lesson 13 Exercise 2 • Pages 131-132			
	Day 63	Complete Lesson 13 Exercise 3 • Pages 133-135			
	Day 64	Complete Lesson 13 Exercise 4 • Page 136			
	Day 65	Complete Lesson 13 Exercise 5 • Pages 137-138			

Date	Day	Assignment	Due Date	✓	Grade
Week 5	Day 66	Read Story • Page 139 Complete Lesson 14 Exercise 1 • Page 140			
	Day 67	Complete Lesson 14 Exercise 2 • Pages 141-142			
	Day 68	Complete Lesson 14 Exercise 3 • Pages 143-145			
	Day 69	Complete Lesson 14 Exercise 4 • Page 146			
	Day 70	Complete Lesson 14 Exercise 5 • Pages 147-148			
Week 6	Day 71	Picture Study • Page 149 Complete Lesson 15 Exercise 1 • Page 150			
	Day 72	Complete Lesson 15 Exercise 2 • Page 151			
	Day 73	Complete Lesson 15 Exercise 3 • Pages 152-153			
	Day 74	Complete Lesson 15 Exercise 4 • Page 154			
	Day 75	Complete Lesson 15 Exercise 5 • Pages 155-156			
Week 7	Day 76	Read Story • Page 157 Complete Lesson 16 Exercise 1 • Page 158			
	Day 77	Complete Lesson 16 Exercise 2 • Pages 159-160			
	Day 78	Complete Lesson 16 Exercise 3 • Pages 161-163			
	Day 79	Complete Lesson 16 Exercise 4 • Page 164			
	Day 80	Complete Lesson 16 Exercise 5 • Pages 165-166			
Week 8	Day 81	Read Psalm 98 • Page 167 Complete Lesson 17 Exercise 1 • Page 168			
	Day 82	Complete Lesson 17 Exercise 2 • Pages 169-170			
	Day 83	Complete Lesson 17 Exercise 3 • Pages 171-173			
	Day 84	Complete Lesson 17 Exercise 4 • Page 174			
	Day 85	Complete Lesson 17 Exercise 5 • Pages 175-176			
Week 9	Day 86	Read Story • Page 177 Complete Lesson 18 Exercise 1 • Page 178			
	Day 87	Do Lesson 18 Exercise 2 (**Quarter 2 Review**) • Pages 179-180			
	Day 88	Do Lesson 18 Exercise 3 (**Quarter 2 Review**) • Pages 181-184			
	Day 89	Complete Lesson 18 Exercise 4 • Page 185			
	Day 90	Complete Lesson 18 Exercise 5 • Page 186			
		Mid-Term Grade			

Second Semester Suggested Daily Schedule

Date	Day	Assignment	Due Date	✓	Grade
		Second Semester-Third Quarter			
Week 1	Day 91	Read Story • Page 187 Complete Lesson 19 Exercise 1 • Page 188			
	Day 92	Complete Lesson 19 Exercise 2 • Pages 189-190			
	Day 93	Complete Lesson 19 Exercise 3 • Page 191			
	Day 94	Complete Lesson 19 Exercise 4 • Page 192			
	Day 95	Complete Lesson 19 Exercise 5 • Pages 193-194			
Week 2	Day 96	Picture Study • Page 195 Complete Lesson 20 Exercise 1 • Page 196			
	Day 97	Complete Lesson 20 Exercise 2 • Pages 197-198			
	Day 98	Complete Lesson 20 Exercise 3 • Page 199			
	Day 99	Complete Lesson 20 Exercise 4 • Page 200			
	Day 100	Complete Lesson 20 Exercise 5 • Pages 201-202			
Week 3	Day 101	Read Story • Page 203 Complete Lesson 21 Exercise 1 • Page 204			
	Day 102	Complete Lesson 21 Exercise 2 • Pages 205-206			
	Day 103	Complete Lesson 21 Exercise 3 • Pages 207-209			
	Day 104	Complete Lesson 21 Exercise 4 • Page 210			
	Day 105	Complete Lesson 21 Exercise 5 • Pages 211-212			
Week 4	Day 106	Read Poem • Page 213 Complete Lesson 22 Exercise 1 • Page 214			
	Day 107	Complete Lesson 22 Exercise 2 • Pages 215-216			
	Day 108	Complete Lesson 22 Exercise 3 • Pages 217-219			
	Day 109	Complete Lesson 22 Exercise 4 • Page 220			
	Day 110	Complete Lesson 22 Exercise 5 • Pages 221-222			
Week 5	Day 111	Read Story • Page 223 Complete Lesson 23 Exercise 1 • Pages 224-225			
	Day 112	Complete Lesson 23 Exercise 2 • Pages 226-227			
	Day 113	Complete Lesson 23 Exercise 3 • Pages 228-229			
	Day 114	Complete Lesson 23 Exercise 4 • Page 230			
	Day 115	Complete Lesson 23 Exercise 5 • Pages 231-232			
Week 6	Day 116	Picture Study • Page 233 Complete Lesson 24 Exercise 1 • Page 234			
	Day 117	Complete Lesson 24 Exercise 2 • Page 235-236			
	Day 118	Complete Lesson 24 Exercise 3 • Pages 237-239			
	Day 119	Complete Lesson 24 Exercise 4 • Page 240			
	Day 120	Complete Lesson 24 Exercise 5 • Pages 241-242			

Date	Day	Assignment	Due Date	✓	Grade
Week 7	Day 121	Read Story • Page 243 Complete Lesson 25 Exercise 1 • Pages 244-245			
	Day 122	Complete Lesson 25 Exercise 2 • Pages 246-247			
	Day 123	Complete Lesson 25 Exercise 3 • Pages 248-249			
	Day 124	Complete Lesson 25 Exercise 4 • Page 250			
	Day 125	Complete Lesson 25 Exercise 5 • Pages 251-252			
Week 8	Day 126	Read Psalm 100 • Page 253 Complete Lesson 26 Exercise 1 • Page 254			
	Day 127	Complete Lesson 26 Exercise 2 • Pages 255-256			
	Day 128	Complete Lesson 26 Exercise 3 • Page 257			
	Day 129	Complete Lesson 26 Exercise 4 • Page 258			
	Day 130	Complete Lesson 26 Exercise 5 • Pages 259-260			
Week 9	Day 131	Read Story • Page 261 Complete Lesson 27 Exercise 1 • Page 262			
	Day 132	Do Lesson 27 Exercise 2 **(Quarter 3 Review)**• Pages 263-265			
	Day 133	Do Lesson 27 Exercise 3 **(Quarter 3 Review)**• Pages 266-268			
	Day 134	Complete Lesson 27 Exercise 4 • Page 269			
	Day 135	Complete Lesson 27 Exercise 5 • Page 270			
Second Semester-Fourth Quarter					
Week 1	Day 136	Read Story • Page 271 Complete Lesson 28 Exercise 1 • Pages 272-273			
	Day 137	Complete Lesson 28 Exercise 2 • Pages 274-276			
	Day 138	Complete Lesson 28 Exercise 3 • Pages 277-279			
	Day 139	Complete Lesson 28 Exercise 4 • Page 280			
	Day 140	Complete Lesson 28 Exercise 5 • Pages 281-282			
Week 2	Day 141	Picture Study • Page 283 Complete Lesson 29 Exercise 1 • Page 284			
	Day 142	Complete Lesson 29 Exercise 2 • Pages 285-286			
	Day 143	Complete Lesson 29 Exercise 3 • Pages 287-289			
	Day 144	Complete Lesson 29 Exercise 4 • Page 290			
	Day 145	Complete Lesson 29 Exercise 5 • Pages 291-292			
Week 3	Day 146	Read Story • Page 293 Complete Lesson 30 Exercise 1 • Pages 294-295			
	Day 147	Complete Lesson 30 Exercise 2 • Pages 296-298			
	Day 148	Complete Lesson 30 Exercise 3 • Page 299			
	Day 149	Complete Lesson 30 Exercise 4 • Page 300			
	Day 150	Complete Lesson 30 Exercise 5 • Pages 301-302			
Week 4	Day 151	Read Poem • Page 303 Complete Lesson 31 Exercise 1 • Page 304			
	Day 152	Complete Lesson 31 Exercise 2 • Pages 305-306			
	Day 153	Complete Lesson 31 Exercise 3 • Page 307			
	Day 154	Complete Lesson 31 Exercise 4 • Page 308			
	Day 155	Complete Lesson 31 Exercise 5 • Pages 309-310			

Date	Day	Assignment	Due Date	✓	Grade
Week 5	Day 156	Read Story • Page 311 Complete Lesson 32 Exercise 1 • Page 312			
	Day 157	Complete Lesson 32 Exercise 2 • Pages 313-315			
	Day 158	Complete Lesson 32 Exercise 3 • Pages 316-317			
	Day 159	Complete Lesson 32 Exercise 4 • Page 318			
	Day 160	Complete Lesson 32 Exercise 5 • Pages 319-320			
Week 6	Day 161	Picture Study • Page 321 Complete Lesson 33 Exercise 1 • Page 322			
	Day 162	Complete Lesson 33 Exercise 2 • Pages 323-325			
	Day 163	Complete Lesson 33 Exercise 3 • Pages 326-327			
	Day 164	Complete Lesson 33 Exercise 4 • Page 328			
	Day 165	Complete Lesson 33 Exercise 5 • Pages 329-330			
Week 7	Day 166	Read Story • Page 331 Complete Lesson 34 Exercise 1 • Page 332			
	Day 167	Complete Lesson 34 Exercise 2 • Pages 333-334			
	Day 168	Complete Lesson 34 Exercise 3 • Page 335			
	Day 169	Complete Lesson 34 Exercise 4 • Page 336			
	Day 170	Complete Lesson 34 Exercise 5 • Pages 337-338			
Week 8	Day 171	Read Psalm 117 • Page 339 Complete Lesson 35 Exercise 1 • Page 340			
	Day 172	Complete Lesson 35 Exercise 2 • Page 341			
	Day 173	Complete Lesson 35 Exercise 3 • Pages 342-343			
	Day 174	Complete Lesson 35 Exercise 4 • Page 344			
	Day 175	Complete Lesson 35 Exercise 5 • Pages 345-346			
Week 9	Day 176	Read Story • Page 347 Complete Lesson 36 Exercise 1 • Page 348			
	Day 177	Do Lesson 36 Exercise 2 **(Quarter 4 Review)**• Pages 349-351			
	Day 178	Do Lesson 36 Exercise 3 **(Quarter 4 Review)**• Pages 352-354			
	Day 179	Complete Lesson 36 Exercise 4 • Page 355			
	Day 180	Complete Lesson 36 Exercise 5 • Page 356			
		Final Grade			

Move Up! Day

It was the first day of the new Sunday school session, and Micah was a bit nervous. He was not really excited about "moving up" to the fourth- and fifth-grade class. He was sad that Jin, who was a year younger than Micah, would be staying in the old class with Mr. Lopez.

As Micah's family was finishing breakfast, his dad reminded him that he would not be the only one feeling nervous today. "It's perfectly normal to feel this way," he said. "Remember that stepping into new situations is part of growing older and a great opportunity to trust God and learn some valuable life lessons. Try to see this as an exciting opportunity. You might even make some new friends." *But I will be the youngest kid in the class!* Micah thought to himself. He was not sure he wanted the "life lessons" that came with growing up.

Then his older sister, Alexia, asked him if he knew who his new teacher would be. Micah was so concerned about being the youngest he had not even considered a new teacher! He really liked Mr. Lopez and was comfortable with him. *What would the new teacher be like? Would he or she be as cool as Mr. Lopez? How many kids would be in his new class? Why did he have to be the youngest? Why does everything have to change?*

Micah had a lot on his mind as he rode to church that morning.

NARRATION PRACTICE

TEACHER NOTE

- Please review Reading and Narration tips at the beginning of the book.

(1) How does this story start?

(2) What did Micah's dad remind him of?

(3) What did Alexia say to Micah? What did this make Micah think about?

(4) How does the story end?

Analogy

An analogy shows a relationship between words. Even though the sets of words are different, they have something in common. Study this example:

day : light : : night : dark

Do you see how the sets of words have something in common? In the day it is light just like at night it is dark. The words *day* and *light* have the same relationship with each other as *night* and *dark*.

The analogy we studied has special symbols that help us to read it.

: means "is to"	:: means "as"
day : light ::	night : dark
day is to light as	night is to dark.

Read this analogy out loud to your teacher:

glove : hand :: sock : foot

An analogy is like a fun puzzle to solve. Remember to study the first two words for clues to solve the analogy of the last two words.

TEACHER NOTE
• Please review reading analogies with the student until they understand the concept and how to read them.

Read and complete the analogies.

(1) **yellow : sun :: green : _____**

(2) **kitten : cat :: puppy : _____**

INDEPENDENT READING

TEACHER NOTE
• See instructions for Independent Reading in the front of the book.
• Discuss with the student who an author is and where the name of the author can be found.

Nouns

A noun is a person, place, or thing. A proper noun names a person, place, or thing. Proper nouns include the days of the week, months, and holidays. A proper noun begins with a capital letter.

Study the chart:

Common Nouns	Proper Nouns	Common Nouns	Proper Nouns
boy	Gideon	day	Friday
park	Yellowstone	holiday	Christmas
country	United States	me	I

Write a proper noun for each common noun.

state _____   girl _____

city _____   book _____

month _____   holiday _____

myself _____

Write a sentence using at least one proper noun.

_____

_____

Sentences

When we write a sentence, we must remember to start the first word of each sentence with a capital letter. We also must remember to end it with a punctuation mark.

There are four types of sentences:

Imperative:	gives a command; ends with a period
Declarative:	makes a statement; ends with a period
Exclamatory:	expresses strong emotion; ends with an exclamation point
Interrogative:	asks a question; ends with a question mark

Correctly match the four types of sentences:

(1) Imperative   asks a question

(2) Declarative   expresses strong emotion

(3) Exclamatory   makes a statement

(4) Interrogative   gives a command

Write the correct punctuation after each sentence type.

(1) Imperative _____

(2) Declarative _____

(3) Exclamatory _____

(4) Interrogative _____

Write an exclamatory sentence.

_____

_____

Write an interrogative sentence.

_____

_____

Write an imperative sentence.

_____

_____

Write a declarative sentence.

_____

_____

Be sure to check your sentences for correct capitalization and punctuation.

READING COMPREHENSION

Read "Israel Demands a King" on pages 82–83 of *101 Favorite Stories from the Bible* with your teacher.

TEACHER NOTE

• Review Reading Tips in the beginning of the book. Students are to give oral answers to the questions in *101 Favorite Stories from the Bible*.

Answer the questions on page 83.

Copy Proverbs 1:25, then memorize it with your teacher.

_____

_____

_____

_____

Copy the picture on page 83. Color your picture.

Copy the caption from page 83.

_____

_____

_____

_____

_____

_____

 **SPELLING PRACTICE**

/a/ Words

We are going to work with words that make the short-a and the long-a sound.

The short-a sound is usually followed by one or two consonants.

The long-a sound can be spelled with: *ay*, *ai*, *a_e*, *ea*, or *ei*

Learn to spell these words:

> break, drain, eight, flake, holiday, jail, past,
> shape, spam, stamp, steak, stray, talent, weigh

The family of /a/ words are going on a trip and need to pack. Group the words by how they are spelled and put them in the right suitcases.

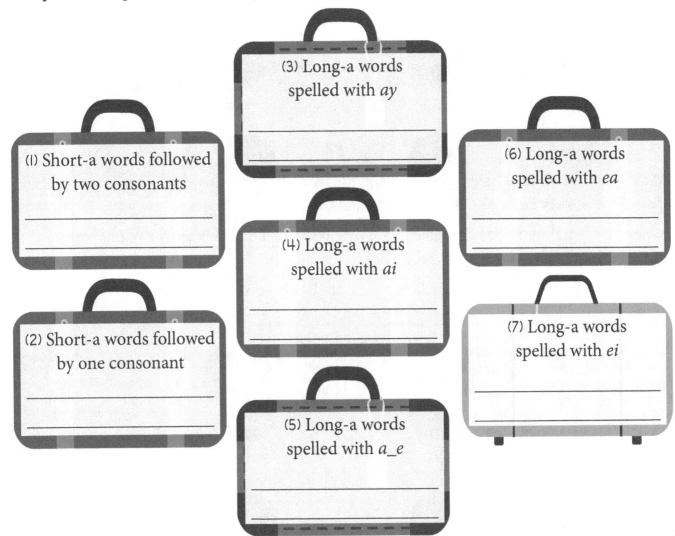

(1) Short-a words followed by two consonants
_____
_____

(2) Short-a words followed by one consonant
_____
_____

(3) Long-a words spelled with *ay*
_____
_____

(4) Long-a words spelled with *ai*
_____
_____

(5) Long-a words spelled with *a_e*
_____
_____

(6) Long-a words spelled with *ea*
_____
_____

(7) Long-a words spelled with *ei*
_____
_____

Write a fun sentence using at least two of your short-a spelling words.

_____

_____

Write a fun sentence using at least two of your long-a spelling words.

_____

_____

Be sure to start each sentence with a capital letter and end it with a punctuation mark.

For More Practice:

 **TEACHER NOTE**
- See note about Spelling and Vocabulary in the front of this book. Extra practice is for students who need more interaction with the spelling words. Assign as needed. Additional games and ideas are also found in the back of the book. Word shape worksheets are also available as a free download.

Write your words in the shape boxes using the worksheet for this lesson available as a free download at masterbooks.com/classroom-aids.

Write your spelling words on notecards. Write one word on each card. You may create right-brain flashcards with your words.

Ask your teacher to read each spelling word. Spell the word out loud and use it in a sentence.

 **CREATE YOUR OWN DICTIONARY!**

 **TEACHER NOTE**
- See instructions for Dictionary in the back of the book.

 **PICTURE STUDY**

Title: Christ and the Children

Artist: Vittorio Bianchini

Scripture Connection

Ask your teacher to read to you Mark 10:13–16 from your Bible.

 **OBSERVATION SKILLS**

(1) Who is in the picture? Describe them.

(2) What is happening in the picture?

(3) How do you think Jesus feels about children?

(4) What colors are used in the picture?

(5) How does this picture make you feel? Why?

(6) What can we learn from this picture and the story it tells?

Sight Words

Read the sight words to your teacher:

TEACHER NOTE • Circle all the words the student must sound out, reads slowly, or needs help reading. Help the student create sight word memory cards as needed. Add to the list any other common words the student has difficulty reading.

apple	bear	birthday	bread	brother
chair	chicken	children	Christmas	door
farmer	father	flower	garden	girl
goodbye	ground	horse	house	kitty
letter	money	morning	mother	night
paper	party	picture	rabbit	robin
school	shoe	sister	squirrel	street
table	thing	watch	water	window

INDEPENDENT READING

Dolch words: The list was prepared in 1936 by Edward William Dolch and was originally published in his book *Problems in Reading* in 1948.

GRAMMAR PRACTICE

Possessive Nouns

A possessive noun shows ownership. We add **'s** to the end of a noun to show that it is a possessive noun.

Example: The tree's leaves are falling.

The leaves that are falling belong to the tree.

Plural means more than one. When a possessive noun is plural and ends with an *s*, we simply add an apostrophe after the *s*.

Example: The trees' leaves are falling.

There is more than one tree with falling leaves. The noun, trees, is plural and ends with an *s*. We added an apostrophe to the *s* to show it is a possessive noun.

Write the possessive form of each noun.

(1) car _____

(2) dog _____

(3) cats _____

(4) bowls _____

Write a sentence using at least one possessive noun.

_____

_____

Write a sentence using at least one plural possessive noun.

_____

_____

Sentences

A sentence must express a complete thought. It must have a subject and a predicate. Remember:

> The subject tells who or what the sentence is about.
> The predicate tells what the subject does or is.

Circle the sentences that are correctly written.

(1) Micah was nervous about his new class?

(2) Dad said Micah would learn a life lesson.

(3) Alexia wanted

(4) micah might make some new friends.

(5) He had a lot on his mind!

Underline the subject and circle the predicate of each sentence.

(6) Micah wanted Jin in his class.

(7) Micah was the youngest in his class.

(8) Micah jumped into the car.

(9) Alexia smiled at him.

Combining sentences is fun, and it helps us share our ideas in a better way. Let's see how it works. Read the two sentences:

> The chicken ran quickly.
> The chicken ran across the yard.

Now let's combine them:

> The chicken ran quickly across the yard.

Now you give it a try!

> Jesus is loving.
> Jesus is kind.

(10) Combine the two sentences into one.

_____

_____

Try it one more time. This one might be tricky!

> The boy read a book.
> The boy read another book.

(11) Combine the two sentences into one.

_____

_____

READING COMPREHENSION

Read "Saul Anointed" on pages 84–85 of *101 Favorite Stories from the Bible* with your teacher.

Answer the questions on page 85.

Copy Psalm 71:16a, then memorize it with your teacher.

_____

_____

_____

_____

Copy the picture on page 85. Color your picture.

Copy the caption from page 85.

_____

_____

_____

_____

_____

_____

 **SPELLING PRACTICE**

/e/ Words

We are going to work with words that make the short-e and the long-e sound. The short-e sound can be spelled with *e* or *ea*. It is usually followed by one or more consonants.

 Exception: The word *been* has a short-e sound and the *ee* pattern.

The long-e sound can be spelled with *ea*, *ee*, *ie* or *y*. Some long-e words end in a silent-e. Learn to spell these words:

> alley, been, chief, desk, east, gently, green
> leather, meant, niece, peach, speed, spent, squeeze

The family of /e/ words are joining the *a* words on their trip and need to pack too. Group the words by how they are spelled and put them in the right suitcases. Two words have already jumped in!

(3) Short-e word spelled with *ee*
_____

(6) Long-e words spelled with *ie*
_____
_____

(1) Long-e words spelled with *y*
alley
gently

(4) Long-e words spelled with *ea*
_____
_____

(7) Short-e words spelled with an *e*
_____
_____

(2) Short-e words spelled with *ea*
_____

(5) Long-e words spelled with *ee* (no silent-e)
_____
_____

(8) Long-e word ending in a silent-e
_____

Write a fun sentence using at least two of your short-e spelling words.

_____

_____

Write a fun sentence using at least two of your long-e spelling words.

_____

_____

Be sure to start each sentence with a capital letter and end it with a punctuation mark.

For More Practice:

Write your words in the shape boxes using the worksheet for this lesson available as a free download at masterbooks.com/classroom-aids.

Write your spelling words on notecards. Write one word on each card. You may create right-brain flashcards with your words.

Ask your teacher to read each spelling word. Spell the word out loud and use it in a sentence.

 CREATE YOUR OWN DICTIONARY!

New Teacher

Claire was waiting for Micah in the hallway. "Hi, Micah!" she said. "I've been waiting for you to get here. Isn't this exciting? I can't wait to see who our new teacher is!" Micah relaxed a little, happy he wouldn't have to walk in by himself. He secretly hoped some of Claire's excitement would rub off on him too.

They found their seats, and Micah noticed several kids walk in who also looked just like he felt. Micah realized his dad had been right about that. Some of the older kids even came over and said hello. *Maybe this would be okay after all.*

At the front of the room was a table covered by a large cloth. You could tell there was something under the covering because of all the lumps and bumps. As he was pondering what it could be, an older gentleman walked through the door and said, "Good morning, class! I'm Mr. Cunningham, but you can call me Mr. C." Micah thought "Mr. C." might be old enough to be his grandfather or even great-grandfather, but he sure seemed excited about something.

After having all the students introduce themselves, he told the class a little about himself. It turns out Mr. C. was a retired architect and had traveled all over the world. "Under this cloth though is the most interesting project I've had the pleasure of working on," he said. Micah's jaw dropped as Mr. C. removed the cloth to reveal an exact replica of Solomon's Temple Complex made out of – LEGOs®!

(1) How does the story start?

(2) Describe what was on the table.

(3) Describe Mr. Cunningham. What did they call him for short?

(4) How does the story end?

Map - Compare It!

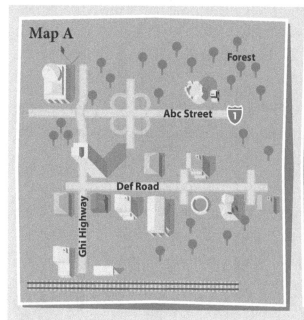
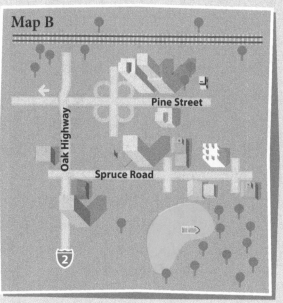
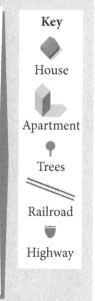

Sometimes you can compare different maps to find different things.
Look at the map key for Map A and Map B. Circle the correct answer.

(1) Which map has a house?   Map A   Map B Both

(2) Which map has an apartment? Map A   Map B Both

(3) On which map is Highway 2?   Map A   Map B Both

(4) On which map is Abc Street?   Map A   Map B Both

(5) Which map has railroad tracks? Map A   Map B Both

Sight Words

Practice the sight words using your memorization cards.

INDEPENDENT
READING

 **GRAMMAR PRACTICE**

Pronouns

Pronouns take the place of one or more nouns.

When a pronoun takes the place of more than one noun, it is called a plural pronoun.

Study the chart:

Singular Pronouns	Plural Pronouns
I, you, it	us
she, her	we
he, him	them

Study the examples:

I am going to a new class.
We are going to a new class.

(1) What is the singular pronoun in the first sentence? _____

(2) What is the plural pronoun in the second sentence? _____

Write a sentence using a singular pronoun.

_____

_____

Write a sentence using a plural pronoun.

_____

_____

The antecedent is the noun or nouns the pronoun stands for.

Copy what an antecedent is.

_____

_____

Study the examples:

Claire and I are going to a new class.
We are going to a new class.

(3) What is the antecedent the pronoun *we* stands for? (**Hint:** The answer has more than one noun.) _____

JUST **4** FUN!

(4) Complete the maze and help Micah get to his new class! You can also trace ahead with your finger before you use a pencil or marker to show the way. (You can only go through the open doors.)

Interjections and Conjunctions

Do you remember what an interjection is? They are words added to a sentence that express emotion. Here are some examples:

Yay! Ouch! Wow! Hurray! Yes! Stop!

Here is an example of how we can use an interjection in a sentence to express emotion:

Ouch! I have a sliver in my finger.

Write a sentence using an interjection.

_____

_____

Do you remember what a conjunction is? It is a word that connects words and phrases. Let's look at some common conjunctions.

for and nor but or yet so

We can memorize this list of common conjunctions by looking at the first letter of each word:

for and nor but or yet so

(1) Write the first letter of each word here:

____ ____ ____ ____ ____ ____ ____

That is a silly word that can help us remember some conjunctions. We call this an **acronym**. An acronym is letters that stand for words. We can use acronyms to help us remember things.

Here is a sentence that includes a conjunction. Look for the conjunction. Do you see the words the conjunction joins together?

Claire and Micah waited in the hallway.

The conjunction *and* joins together the two words Claire, Micah. Let's read the same sentence without the conjunction.

Claire Micah waited in the hallway.

That sounds a bit silly, doesn't it? Conjunctions help us to write good sentences.

Now you try it. Write a sentence using a conjunction.

_____

_____

(2) Do you remember the acronym fanboys? Write the conjunctions. Try to remember them without looking back!

F _____

A _____

N _____

B _____

O _____

Y _____

S _____

JUST **4** FUN!

Details, Details!

(3) Mr. C. used to design houses and buildings. To be an architect, you have to pay attention to details. See if you can spot and circle the two identical pictures of birdhouses.

1

2

3

4

5

6

7

8

9

Read "David — The Shepherd Boy" on pages 86–87 of *101 Favorite Stories from the Bible* with your teacher.

Answer the questions on page 87.

Copy Romans 13:1b, then memorize it with your teacher.

_____

_____

_____

_____

Copy the picture on page 87. Color your picture.

Copy the caption from page 87.

_____

_____

_____

_____

_____

_____

 SPELLING PRACTICE

/i/ Words

We are going to work with words that make the short-i and the long-i sound.

The short-i sound can be spelled with *i* and is often followed by one or more consonants.

The long-i sound can be spelled with: *i*, *igh*, *i_e*, or *y*.

Watch these tricky /i/ words:

 ruin, build, diet, height, align, type

Learn to spell these words:

align, build, deny, diet, flight, grind, height,
inch, pilot, ruin, shine, sting, thigh, type

The family of /i/ words were invited to join the *a* and *e* words on their trip, and now they need to pack. Group the words by how they are spelled and put them in the right suitcases.

(5) Long-i word spelled with *y*
_____

(1) Short-i words spelled with an *i*
_____
_____

(3) Long-i word spelled with *i_e*
_____

(6) Long-i word spelled with an *i*
_____
_____

(4) Long-i tricky words
_____
_____
_____

(2) Short-i tricky words
_____
_____

(7) Long-i words spelled with *igh*
_____
_____

Write a fun sentence using at least two of your short-i spelling words.

_____

_____

Write a fun sentence using at least two of your long-i spelling words.

_____

_____

Be sure to start each sentence with a capital letter and end it with a punctuation mark.

For More Practice:

Write your words in the shape boxes using the worksheet for this lesson available as a free download at masterbooks.com/classroom-aids.

Write your spelling words on notecards. Write one word on each card. You may create right-brain flashcards with your words.

Ask your teacher to read each spelling word. Spell the word out loud and use it in a sentence.

CREATE YOUR OWN DICTIONARY!

A White Hen Sitting

By Christina Georgina Rossetti

A white hen sitting
On white eggs three:
Next, three speckled chickens
As plump as plump can be.
An owl, and a hawk,
And a bat come to see:
But chicks beneath their mother's wing
Squat safe as safe can be.

Comprehension

Were there any words you didn't understand? Circle them.

TEACHER NOTE

• The teacher should go over with the student the meaning of the circled words in the context of the poem.

NARRATION PRACTICE

(1) Who wrote the poem?

(2) What is the poem about?

(3) Why do you think the author wrote this poem?

(4) Explain how this poem makes you feel.

Rossetti, Christina. (1893). *Sing-Song: A Nursery Rhyme Book.* New York: MacMillan and Co., p. 86.

Memorization

Memorize the poem with your teacher.

Sight Words

Practice sight words using your memorization cards.

Animal Sudoku

(1) Each animal can only appear in each line of boxes one time. Your challenge is to find where the animal cards at the bottom go. Cut them out carefully, and then place them in a row. Then look at the rows it is in (up and down, left and right) and see if that animal is already in the line. If it is, you have to try a different animal card. If not, leave it there and see if you can complete the row.

cut and glue

GRAMMAR PRACTICE

Possessive Pronouns

Do you remember what possessive means? It means ownership.

Do you remember adding an *apostrophe* or an *apostrophe s* to nouns to make them possessive? We do not do this for pronouns. We simply use **possessive pronouns**.

Study the chart:

Possessive Pronouns
my, his, her, its, our, your, their

Study the example:

It is my class.

(1) What is the possessive pronoun? _____

(2) What belongs to the possessive pronoun? _____

Copy the lists of possessive pronouns.

_____

_____

Write a sentence using a possessive pronoun.

_____

_____

What possessive pronoun did you use in your sentence? _____

What belongs to the possessive pronoun you used? _____

Some possessive pronouns can stand alone. What belongs to the possessive pronoun does not have to follow it.

Study the chart:

> ## Pronouns that can Stand Alone
> ### mine, yours, ours, his, hers, theirs

Note: The pronoun *his* can be used with a regular possessive pronoun, and it can stand alone.

We are going to use the pronoun *his* in two ways. Study the examples:

Mr. C. showed us his Temple.

In this sentence, the pronoun *his* is used to show ownership of the Temple.

It is his.

In this sentence, the pronoun *his* stands alone.

Copy the list of pronouns that can stand alone.

_____

_____

Write a sentence using a pronoun that can stand alone.

_____

_____

Sentences

Do you remember what the subject and predicate is of a sentence? The subject of a sentence tells who or what the sentence is about. The predicate of a sentence tells us something about the subject.

Compound means more than one. We can have a compound subject. Here is an example to study:

An owl and bat came to see the chicks.

(1) What is the subject of this sentence? (**Hint:** There is more than one noun in the subject.)

_____

Did you notice the conjunction in that compound subject?

(2) What was it? _____

Conjunctions sure are helpful!

Write a sentence with a compound subject. You can do it!

_____

_____

Compound predicates work the same way as compound subjects. Here is an example:

The chicken sat and hatched the three eggs.

I spotted another conjunction in that compound sentence. Did you see it?

(3) What was it? _____

(4) Write the compound predicate.

_____

Write a sentence with a compound predicate. You can do it!

_____

_____

Compound subjects and predicates make our sentences more interesting. They can even save us time! Do you want to know how? Let's make a little story out of our example sentences.

Read the story to your teacher.

> The chicken sat and hatched the three eggs.
> An owl and bat came to see the chicks.

Now, let's see what the story would look like if we didn't use compound subjects and predicates.

Read the story to your teacher.

> The chicken sat on three eggs.
> The chicken hatched the three eggs.
> An owl came to see the chicks.
> A bat came to see the chicks.

Which story did you read the quickest?

Which story would you want to write down as copy work?

Which story sounded better?

I sure like using compound subjects and predicates. Do you?

Lost and Found!

(5) See if you can help the chick find its mother.

Read "David and Goliath" on pages 88–89 of *101 Favorite Stories from the Bible* with your teacher.

Answer the questions on page 89.

Copy Psalm 147:11, then memorize it with your teacher.

_____

_____

_____

_____

Copy the picture on page 89. Color your picture.

Copy the caption from page 89.

_____

_____

_____

_____

_____

_____

SPELLING PRACTICE

/o/ Words

We are going to work with words that make the short-o and the long-o sound.

The short-o sound can be spelled with *o* and is usually followed by one or more consonants.

The long-o sound can be spelled with: *o, oa, o_e,* or *ow*.

Learn to spell these words:

> broke, coast, crow, globe, goal, gold, growth,
> host, problem, shock, shop, shown, snow, wrote

The family of /o/ words were invited to join the *a*, *e*, and *i* words on their trip and now they need to pack. Group the words by how they are spelled and put them in the right suitcases.

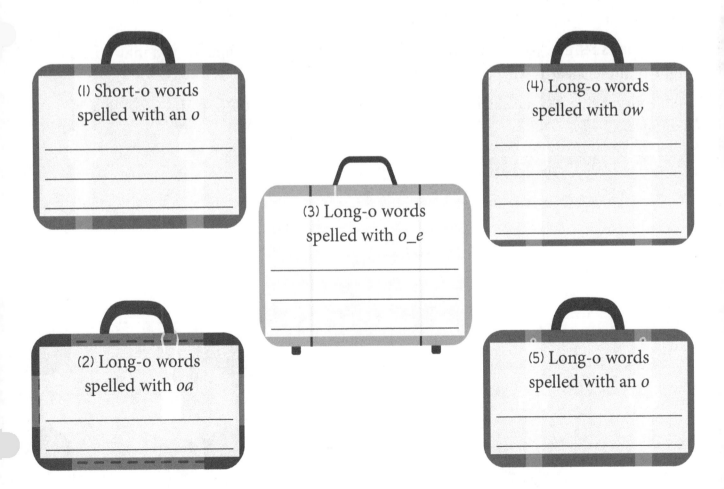

(1) Short-o words spelled with an *o*

_____
_____
_____

(4) Long-o words spelled with *ow*

_____
_____
_____

(3) Long-o words spelled with *o_e*

_____
_____
_____

(2) Long-o words spelled with *oa*

_____
_____

(5) Long-o words spelled with an *o*

_____
_____

Write a fun sentence using at least two of your short-o spelling words.

_____

_____

Write a fun sentence using at least two of your long-o spelling words.

_____

_____

Be sure to start each sentence with a capital letter and end it with a punctuation mark.

For More Practice:

Write your words in the shape boxes using the worksheet for this lesson available as a free download at masterbooks.com/classroom-aids.

Write your spelling words on notecards. Write one word on each card. You may create right-brain flashcards with your words.

Ask your teacher to read each spelling word. Spell the word out loud and use it in a sentence.

 CREATE YOUR OWN DICTIONARY!

Solomon's Temple

Micah had told Jin all about the LEGO® version of Solomon's Temple. They ran to Micah's class, hoping to get a peek at it. Mr. Cunningham uncovered his creation as he told the boys about the books he studied to make sure the details were all correct. Jin laughed at the little capes on the LEGO® men in the outer court. Micah sure missed Jin, but he was thankful Mr. C. showed them Solomon's Temple. The boys said their thanks, then waved a quick goodbye as Jin headed off to his own class.

Micah got lost in thought as he studied the LEGO® Temple. He imagined the people in Bible days visiting the Temple on the Sabbath, which he had learned about in his Sunday school class with Mr. Lopez. God had told His people to rest on the seventh day of each week, just as He had done the week He created the world. Micah also remembered the ram's horn Mr. Lopez had blown when they learned about the Feast of Trumpets, another holy day God set aside for His people to celebrate.

As Claire came up behind him, Micah jumped. Claire laughed and reminded Micah it was time for class to start. They both took a seat, but Micah couldn't take his eyes off the Temple. He had so many questions for Mr. C. *How long did it take to complete? Why did Mr. C. build it? Where did Mr. C. keep it when it wasn't on display in class?*

NARRATION PRACTICE

(1) How does the story begin?

(2) What did Micah imagine while looking at Solomon's Temple?

(3) How does the story end?

Memorization

Mr. Lopez told the class that the Feast of Trumpets is described in Leviticus 23:24.

> "Speak to the sons of Israel, saying, 'In the seventh month on the first of the month you shall have a rest, a reminder by blowing of trumpets, a holy convocation."

Memorize the verse with your teacher.

Sight Words

Do you know all the sight words yet? If not, keep practicing them with your teacher at least once a week.

Sequencing

(I)   Put the stories in order by writing the correct number under each picture.

Micah woke up early.
First, Micah brushed his teeth.
Next, Micah got dressed.
Micah ate his breakfast before he left for church.

 **GRAMMAR PRACTICE**

Verbs

Do you remember what an action verb is? It tells what is happening in a sentence.

Mr. Lopez blew the ram's horn.

(1) What is the action verb in this sentence? _____

Action verbs bring our sentences to life. There are many action verbs to choose from. Let's see how we can change a sentence by using a different action verb in the same sentence.

Micah hopped when Claire surprised him.
Micah jumped when Claire surprised him.
Micah leaped when Claire surprised him.

We used a word that means almost the same thing in each of the sentences, but each one changed the picture we have in our mind.

Let's see what happens if we use action verbs that have different meanings in the same sentence.

Micah screamed when Claire surprised him.
Micah ran when Claire surprised him.
Micah sneezed when Claire surprised him.

Even though we used the same sentence, changing the action verb changes what we see in our mind as we read it. You can see how careful we should be when choosing an action verb!

Let's have some fun. Make a list of four action verbs.

_____   _____   _____   _____

Write a sentence using the first action verb.

_____

_____

Write the same sentence using the second action verb.

_____

_____

Write the same sentence using the third action verb.

_____

_____

Write the same sentence using the fourth action verb.

_____

_____

Which sentence is your favorite? Tell your teacher a short story, starting with your favorite sentence.

Discuss with your teacher how your story may have changed if you had used one of the other sentences.

Quotation Marks

A quotation is when you copy exactly what someone has said. Study this example:

> Claire said, "It is time for class to start."

Did you notice the funny little marks at the start and end of the quote? Those are called **quotation marks**. They let us know the exact words someone has said.

When we use a quote in a sentence, there are few things we need to make sure we do.

Use quotation marks before and after the quote.

Use a comma after the last word before the quotation.

Use a capital letter to start the quotation.

But what if the quote comes first? Study this example:

> "It is time for class to start," Claire said.

Did you notice the comma at the end of the quote? We can add a new rule to our list:

> If a quote comes before the person who spoke, use a comma after the quote and before the ending quotation marks.

Let's practice quotation marks. Add the correct punctuation to the sentences that use quotations. Study the examples and our list of hints if you aren't sure.

(1) Micah said Jin, come see the Temple in my class.

(2) It took a long time to build this Temple said Mr. C.

Now it is your turn! Write a sentence using a quotation.

_____

_____

READING COMPREHENSION

Read "David's Wise Behavior" on pages 90–91 of *101 Favorite Stories from the Bible* with your teacher.

Answer the questions on page 91.

Copy Psalm 115:13, then memorize it with your teacher.

_____

_____

_____

_____

Copy the picture on page 91. Color your picture.

Copy the caption from page 91.

_____

_____

_____

_____

_____

_____

 **SPELLING PRACTICE**

/u/ Words

We are going to work with words that make the short-u, long-u, and the /oo/ sound.

The short-u sound can be spelled with *u* and is usually followed by one or more consonants.

The long-u sound can be spelled with *u, ue, u_e,* or *ew*.

The /oo/ sound can be spelled with *oo, ou, u, u_e, ew,* or *ui*.

Watch these tricky /u/ words:

> prove, done

Learn to spell these words:

> cute, done, fruit, glue, group, nephew, prove,
> punish, rescue, smooth, threw, truth, tube, unit

The family of /u/ words were invited to join the *a, e, i* and *o* words on their trip and now they need to pack. Group the words by how they are spelled and put them in the right suitcases.

(3) Long-u word spelled with *ew*
_____

(6) Long-u word spelled with a *u*
_____

(1) Short-u word spelled with a *u*
_____

(4) Long-u word spelled with *ue*
_____

(7) /oo/ word spelled with *oo*
_____

(2) Short-u tricky word
_____

(5) Long-u word spelled with *u_e*
_____

(8) /oo/ word spelled with *ou*
_____

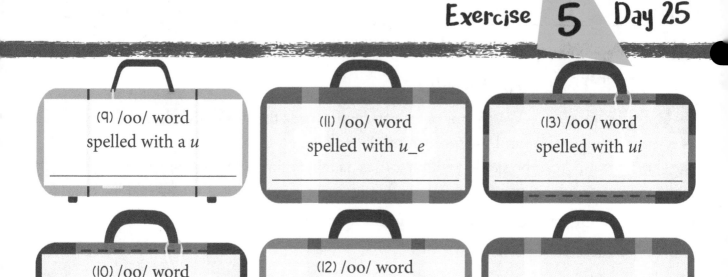

(9) /oo/ word spelled with a *u*

_____

(11) /oo/ word spelled with *u_e*

_____

(13) /oo/ word spelled with *ui*

_____

(10) /oo/ word spelled with *ue*

_____

(12) /oo/ word spelled with *ew*

_____

(14) /oo/ tricky word

_____

Write a fun sentence using at least two of your spelling words.

_____

_____

Write a fun sentence using at least two more of your spelling words.

_____

_____

Be sure to start each sentence with a capital letter and end it with a punctuation mark.

For More Practice:

Write your words in the shape boxes using the worksheet for this lesson available as a free download at masterbooks.com/classroom-aids.

Write your spelling words on notecards. Write one word on each card. You may create right-brain flashcards with your words.

Ask your teacher to read each spelling word. Spell the word out loud and use it in a sentence.

CREATE YOUR OWN DICTIONARY!

Title: One of the Family

Artist: Frederick George Cotman

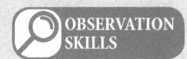 **OBSERVATION SKILLS**

(1) Who is the artist of this picture?

(2) What is happening in the picture?

(3) What are some of the things you see on the table?

(4) Who do you see in the background?

(5) What colors are used in this picture?

(6) How does this picture make you feel? Why?

Story Writing

Finish this story based on the picture.

> All the children came running for dinner. It smelled so good! They quickly took a seat.

_____

_____

_____

_____

_____

_____

INDEPENDENT READING

GRAMMAR PRACTICE

State of Being Verbs

Do you remember the eight **state of being verbs**? They are:

| is | am | are | was | were | be | been | being |

Memorize the state of being verbs if you haven't already.

State of being verbs show state of being rather than action. They link the subject to the predicate. Here is a sentence using a state of being verb.

Micah and Jin are happy.

The linking verb *are* links the subject *Micah and Jin* to the predicate *happy*. Without the state of being verb *are*, the sentence wouldn't make any sense or sound right.

Write a sentence using one of the state of being verbs.

_____

_____

There is another type of verb called **helping verbs**. Helping verbs help another verb in a sentence. They come before the main verb.

Study the helping verbs:

has	have	had		do	does	did
can	will	shall		could	would	should
must	may	might				

Memorize the helping verbs.

Study this example of a helping verb in a sentence:

Micah will bring Jin to his class.

The helping verb is *will*. The verb it helps is *bring*. Together, the helping verb and verb *will bring* show us what is happening in the sentence. They make a great team!

Now it is your turn! Write a sentence using a helping verb.

_____

_____

The eight state of being verbs we learned can be helping verbs too! They also can be used with another verb to link the subject with the predicate. Here is an example:

Micah is bringing Jin to his class.

We changed our sentence just by changing the helping verb and verb team. We used one of our eight state of being verbs as a helping verb. The helping verb *is* works with the verb *bringing* to link the subject and predicate.

Now it is your turn! Write a sentence using one of the eight state of being verbs as a helping verb.

_____

_____

Circle the helping verb in each sentence.

(1) The children should wash their hands.

(2) The family will eat supper soon.

(3) They must pray before they eat.

(4) They might eat pie for dessert.

(5) Dad shall wash the dishes.

Commas

We use a comma when we write a list of things in a sentence. A comma comes after each item in a list except the last item. Study the commas in this sentence and then circle them:

The family had chicken, green beans, and bread for dinner.

Write a sentence with a list separated by commas.

_____

_____

We also use a comma when we address someone. When the person's name is first in a sentence, the comma goes after the name:

Mr. Cunningham, please show us Solomon's Temple.

When the name comes in the middle of the sentence, a comma goes before and after the name:

You, Jin, come closer so you can see.

When the name comes at the end of the sentence, a comma goes before the name:

Isn't this amazing, Micah?

Put commas where they go in the sentences.

(1) Does Claire know about the Temple Micah?

(2) Claire did you see the Temple?

(3) How long Mr. Cunningham did it take to build?

READING COMPREHENSION

Read "Jonathan and David" on pages 92–93 of *101 Favorite Stories from the Bible* with your teacher.

Answer the questions on page 93.

Copy Psalm 145:20, then memorize it with your teacher.

_____

_____

_____

_____

Copy the picture on page 93. Color your picture.

Copy the caption from page 93.

_____

_____

_____

_____

_____

_____

/aw/ and /ow/ Sound Words

We are going to work with words that make the /aw/ and the /ow/ sound.

The /aw/ sound can be spelled with *al*, *au*, and *aw*.

The /ow/ sound can be spelled with *ou* or *ow*.

Some /aw/ and /ow/ sound words end with a silent *e*.

Learn to spell these words:

> **crawl, drawn, exalt, false, faucet, fault, frown, howl, launch, mount, pounce, sauce, sound, sprout**

The /aw/ and /ow/ words were invited to join the fun letter trip, and now they need to pack. Group the words by how they are spelled and put them in the right suitcases.

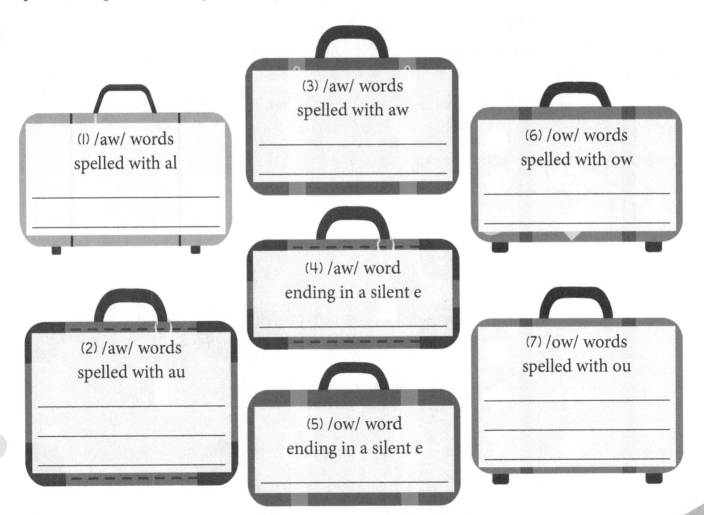

(1) /aw/ words spelled with al

_____
_____

(3) /aw/ words spelled with aw

_____
_____

(6) /ow/ words spelled with ow

_____
_____

(4) /aw/ word ending in a silent e

_____

(2) /aw/ words spelled with au

_____
_____

(5) /ow/ word ending in a silent e

_____

(7) /ow/ words spelled with ou

_____
_____

Write a fun sentence using at least two of your /aw/ spelling words.

_____

_____

Write a fun sentence using at least two of your /ow/ spelling words.

_____

_____

Be sure to start each sentence with a capital letter and end it with a punctuation mark.

For More Practice:

Write your words in the shape boxes using the worksheet for this lesson available as a free download at masterbooks.com/classroom-aids.

Write your spelling words on notecards. Write one word on each card. You may create right-brain flashcards with your words.

Ask your teacher to read each spelling word. Spell the word out loud and use it in a sentence.

 **CREATE YOUR OWN DICTIONARY!**

Micah's Journal

After he got home from church, Micah looked up the verses he wrote down in his journal about the holy days he learned about in Mr. Lopez's class last year. Solomon's Temple had gotten him thinking about the people going to the Temple to celebrate. As he read from Genesis 2:2–3 and Exodus 20, he tried to imagine the people celebrating the Sabbath at the Temple. He couldn't help but chuckle as he thought about those funny LEGO® men with capes.

Next, Micah read about the Day of Atonement. He had written down Leviticus 23:26–32 in his notes. As he looked up the Scripture verses, he remembered how sad Mr. Lopez had been when he talked about this holiday. It was a day to remember the cost of sin and to thank God for sending Jesus.

Mr. Lopez said the last of the fall holy days was found in Leviticus 23. The Feast of Tabernacles was when the people lived in a tent for a whole week! Micah looked up Zechariah 14:16, where it says all nations will someday celebrate this special time. He wondered if it would be anything like the week his family spent camping in a tent last summer.

As Micah read through his journal, he thought about how much he missed Jin in his new class. Then a smile came across his face as he thought about Solomon's Temple. Micah and Jin couldn't stop talking about it after church. Both boys wanted to learn more about the Temple. Micah couldn't wait for his next class!

NARRATION PRACTICE

(1) How does the story begin?

(2) What holy days did Micah remember?

(3) How does the story end?

TEACHER NOTE
- You may want to look up the Scriptures mentioned in the story and read them with the student. You may also read more about the Day of Atonement in Leviticus 23:26–32.

Observation

Study the picture.

Think of a story to go with the picture.

Tell the story to your teacher.

Write your story in four or more sentences by answering the questions.

How does your story start?

_____

_____

What happens next?

_____

_____

What happens after that?

_____

_____

How does your story end?

_____

_____

Verbs

Do you remember the kinds of verbs we have studied? There are action verbs, state of being verbs, and helping verbs.

State of being verbs link a subject with the predicate in a sentence.

Helping verbs help another verb in a sentence. They come before the main verb.

If you haven't done it already, memorize these two types of verbs.

State of Being Verbs

is	am	are	was	were	be	been	being

Helping Verbs

has	have	had	do	does	did
can	will	shall	could	would	should
must	may	might			

Did you know that sometimes state of being verbs are also helping verbs? Sometimes they come before the main verb in a sentence.

Using the lists of verbs, write either a state of being verb or a helping verb in each sentence.

(1) Micah _____ writing in his journal.

(2) The Temple _____ reminded Micah of the holy days.

(3) Micah _____ enjoy sleeping in a tent for a week.

(4) Micah and Jin _____ looking forward to seeing Solomon's Temple again.

Circle the helping verb and underline the main verb in each sentence.

(5) Micah does play with building blocks.

(6) Jin will help Micah.

(7) Micah and Jin should clean the room first.

(8) The boys might build a tent with their building blocks.

(9) The boys were building the tower quickly.

Bonus question:

(10) Which sentence used a state of being verb as a helping verb?

_____

Write a sentence using a state of being verb.

_____

_____

Write a sentence using a helping verb.

_____

_____

Titles of Books, Magazines, Movies, and Plays

When you write a sentence using the title of a book, magazine, movie, or play, you should:

○ Underline the title (or use italics if you are using a computer)

○ Capitalize the first and last word

○ Capitalize all other words except small words that are not nouns, verbs, or adjectives such as: *the, for, and*

Study this example:

> Have you read <u>Whale of a Story</u> by Buddy Davis?

Underline the titles in the sentences below.

(1) Dinosaurs by Design has a lot of good information.

(2) I was in a play called The Christmas Story.

(3) Have you watched A Jurassic Ark Mystery by Buddy Davis?

Write the names of the book, movie, or play correctly.

(4) swamp man! _____

(5) life in the great ice age _____

(6) the flood of noah _____

(7) i dig dinosaurs _____

Write a sentence using the title of a book, movie, or play.

_____

_____

READING COMPREHENSION

Read "King Solomon" on pages 94–95 of *101 Favorite Stories from the Bible* with your teacher.

Answer the questions on page 95.

Copy James 1:5, then memorize it with your teacher.

_____

_____

_____

_____

Copy the picture on page 95. Color your picture.

Copy the caption from page 95.

_____

_____

_____

_____

_____

_____

_____

 **SPELLING PRACTICE**

More /aw/ and /ow/ Sound Words

We are going to work with more words that make the /aw/ and the /ow/ sound.

The /aw/ sound can be spelled with *aught* and *ought*.

The /ow/ sound can be spelled with *ound*.

Learn to spell these words:

> astound, bought, brought, caught, daughter, fought, found, fraught, ground, hound, ought, sought, taught, thought

The new /aw/ and /ow/ words were invited to join the fun letter trip, and now they need to pack. Group the words by how they are spelled and put them in the right suitcases.

(1) /aw/ words spelled with aught

_____
_____
_____

(2) /aw/ words spelled with ought

_____
_____
_____
_____
_____

(3) /ow/ words spelled with ound

_____
_____
_____

Write a fun sentence using at least two of your /aw/ spelling words.

_____

_____

Write a fun sentence using at least two of your /ow/ spelling words.

_____

_____

Be sure to start each sentence with a capital letter and end it with a punctuation mark.

For More Practice:

Write your words in the shape boxes using the worksheet for this lesson available as a free download at masterbooks.com/classroom-aids.

Write your spelling words on notecards. Write one word on each card. You may create right-brain flashcards with your words.

Ask your teacher to read each spelling word. Spell the word out loud and use it in a sentence.

CREATE YOUR OWN DICTIONARY!

Psalm 96

¹Sing to the Lᴏʀᴅ a new song;
Sing to the Lᴏʀᴅ, all the earth.
²Sing to the Lᴏʀᴅ, bless His name;
Proclaim good tidings of His salvation from
    day to day.
³Tell of His glory among the nations,
His wonderful deeds among all the peoples.

⁴For great is the Lᴏʀᴅ and greatly to be
    praised;
He is to be feared above all gods.
⁵For all the gods of the peoples are idols,
But the Lᴏʀᴅ made the heavens.
⁶Splendor and majesty are before Him,
Strength and beauty are in His sanctuary.

⁷Ascribe to the Lᴏʀᴅ, O families of the
    peoples,
Ascribe to the Lᴏʀᴅ glory and strength.
⁸Ascribe to the Lᴏʀᴅ the glory of His name;
Bring an offering and come into His courts.

⁹Worship the Lᴏʀᴅ in holy attire;
Tremble before Him, all the earth.
¹⁰Say among the nations, "The Lᴏʀᴅ reigns;
Indeed, the world is firmly established, it
    will not be moved;
He will judge the peoples with equity."

¹¹Let the heavens be glad, and let the earth
    rejoice;
Let the sea roar, and all it contains;
¹²Let the field exult, and all that is in it.
Then all the trees of the forest will sing
    for joy

¹³Before the Lᴏʀᴅ, for He is coming,
For He is coming to judge the earth.
He will judge the world in righteousness
And the peoples in His faithfulness.

TEACHER NOTE
• Please review tips on reading psalms at the beginning of the book.

Comprehension

A psalm is a song. There are 150 psalms in the Bible. Many of them were written by David.

Were there any words you didn't understand? Circle them.

TEACHER NOTE
• The teacher should go over with the student the meaning of the circled words in the context of the poem.

NARRATION PRACTICE

(1) What chapter of Psalms did you read?

(2) How many verses are there in this chapter?

(3) What was this psalm about?

(4) What did you learn about God in this psalm?

(5) What were your favorite verses?

Memorization

Memorize at least three verses of this psalm. The verses should be in a row and may be picked by you or your teacher.

Syllables

Pick at least two verses of Psalm 96. Read the verses to your teacher. As you read each word, clap for each syllable.

INDEPENDENT READING

Verbs

We have learned about action verbs, state of being verbs (which sometimes are helping verbs), and helping verbs. We have one more kind of verb to study, **linking verbs**.

Linking verbs link a noun or adjective to the subject of the sentence. When state of being verbs aren't acting like helping verbs, they are a linking verb. Here are some examples to study:

State of being helping verb:

I am driving to the store.

The word *am* is the state of being verb. The word *driving* is the main verb it is helping.

State of being linking verb:

Micah and Jin are good friends.

In this sentence, the state of being verb *are* links words *good friends* to the subject *Micah and Jin*.

Tell whether the state of being verb is used as a helping verb or linking verb.

If it is a helping verb, write **H** after the sentence.

If it is a linking verb, write **L** after the sentence. (**Hint:** Remember, helping verbs help the main verb in a sentence.)

(1) Micah is writing in his journal. _____

(2) The Temple was huge. _____

(3) Micah and Claire were running to class. _____

(4) Micah and Claire are best friends. _____

Remember, the state of being verbs are:

> **is   am   are   was   were   be   been   being**

Write a sentence using a state of being verb as a helping verb.

_____

_____

Write a sentence using a state of being verb as a linking verb.

_____

_____

Writing a Paragraph

A **paragraph** is a group of sentences about a specific idea, or topic. A paragraph should:

- ○ Start on a new line with an indent

- ○ Include at least four sentences

- ○ Start with a topic sentence

- ○ Include 2–3 sentences that give details about the topic

- ○ End with a concluding sentence. It ends the paragraph by saying the topic in another way.

Here is an example:

TOPIC SENTENCE

INDENT

Micah read his old journal. He was reminded of the lessons he learned in Sunday school. He remembered the holy days Mr. Lopez talked about. He also remembered how much fun he had with Jin in his class. Micah was glad he kept a journal.

DETAIL SENTENCES

CONCLUDING SENTENCE

Writing a paragraph is like making a sandwich. You use a piece of bread for the top and bottom with the good stuff in between.

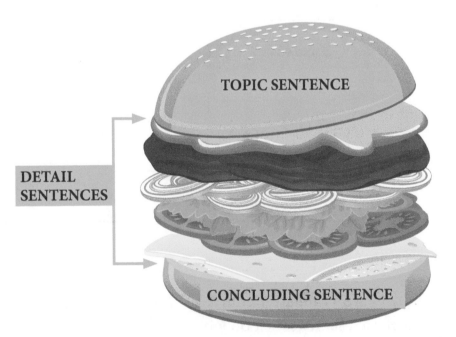

TOPIC SENTENCE

DETAIL SENTENCES

CONCLUDING SENTENCE

Write a paragraph about something you like to do. It can be about a class, writing in a journal, swimming, playing a sport, or any other activity you enjoy. Check off each part as you write your paragraph:

○ Write the topic sentence. Remember to indent your topic sentence.

○ Write 2–3 sentences that give details about your topic. (**Hint:** Some things you like about this activity.)

○ Write a concluding sentence.

_____

_____

_____

_____

_____

_____

_____

_____

_____

_____

Did you use a capital letter to start each sentence? Did you use correct punctuation at the end of each sentence? Good job!

Picture Punctuation!

Draw a smiley face to reflect the emotion in each of the following:

(1) My brother broke my toy! ◯

(2) Where did I leave my socks? ◯

(3) I won a spelling bee! ◯

(4) That was the best joke ever! ◯

(5) I lost my little dog. ◯

(6) This movie is taking too long. ◯

READING COMPREHENSION

Read "Building a Temple for God" on pages 96–97 of *101 Favorite Stories from the Bible* with your teacher.

Answer the questions on page 97.

Copy Psalm 122:1, then memorize it with your teacher.

_____

_____

_____

_____

Copy the picture on page 97. Color your picture.

Copy the caption from page 97.

_____

_____

_____

_____

_____

_____

/r/ Words

We are going to work with /r/ words.

The /ar/ as in car sound cán be spelled with *ar*.

The /ar/ as in air sound can be spelled with *air* and *are*.

The /er/ sound can be spelled with *ir*, *er*, *ur*, *ear*, and *our*.

The /er/ as in ear sound can be spelled with *ear* or *eer*.

The /or/ sound words can be spelled with *or*, *ore*, and *our*.

Learn to spell these words:

> appear, board, career, course, dairy, declare, journey,
> learn, perhaps, purpose, score, sharp, twirl, worn

The /r/ words were invited to join the fun letter trip, and now they need to pack. Group the words by how they are spelled and put them in the right suitcases.

(I) /ar/ as in car; word spelled with ar

_____

(3) /er/ words spelled with ir, er, and ur

_____
_____
_____

(5) /er/ as in ear; words spelled with ear and eer

_____
_____

(2) /ar/ as in air; words spelled with air and are

_____
_____

(4) /er/ as in earn; words spelled with ear and our

_____
_____

(6) /or/ words spelled with or, oar, ore, and our

_____
_____
_____

Write a fun sentence using at least two of your /ar/ spelling words.

_____

_____

Write a fun sentence using at least two of your /er/ spelling words.

_____

_____

Write a fun sentence using at least two of your /or/ spelling words.

_____

_____

Be sure to start each sentence with a capital letter and end it with a punctuation mark.

For More Practice:

Write your words in the shape boxes using the worksheet for this lesson available as a free download at masterbooks.com/classroom-aids.

Write your spelling words on notecards. Write one word on each card. You may create right-brain flashcards with your words.

Ask your teacher to read each spelling word. Spell the word out loud and use it in a sentence.

 CREATE YOUR OWN DICTIONARY!

Trust in the Lord

On Sunday, Mr. C. explained each section of the temple complex and how it was used. "This is a replica of the first temple constructed in Jerusalem and was built by Solomon, the son of King David. Its completion gave the Israelites a permanent place to worship for the first time. There are many lessons we can learn from the life of King Solomon, but one, in particular, is very important. He was fairly young when he became king, but he loved and followed the Lord. Instead of praying for wealth or a long life, he asked instead for wisdom to rule the kingdom well. He built this magnificent temple and encouraged the Israelites to worship the Lord with all their hearts. He started out very strong. Unfortunately, in his later years, he wandered away from God. He began to trust his own judgment instead of trusting the word of God. Sadly, many of the Israelites followed his example. This eventually led to the destruction of this temple by the Babylonians in 586 B.C. I built this replica as a reminder to myself to seek the Lord and His wisdom first, instead of going my own way."

Claire volunteered to read aloud the Scripture Mr. C. chose for today's lesson, Proverbs 3:5–6. "Trust in the LORD with all your heart, and do not lean on your own understanding. In all your ways acknowledge him, and He will make your paths straight."

Micah couldn't help thinking that just a few weeks ago he had wanted to go his own way.

NARRATION PRACTICE

(1) What did Mr. C. explain about Solomon's Temple?

(2) Why did Mr. C. build the replica of Solomon's Temple?

(3) What do you think Micah was thinking about? Do you remember when he wanted to go his own way?

Rhyming

ABAB rhymes are when the two "A" lines rhyme and the two "B" lines rhyme. Let's look at an example:

> A: It is just about time
> B: and I can't wait
> A: to read a rhyme
> B: I can't be late!

The A lines rhyme with each other, and the B lines rhyme with each other. It is a fun way to write a poem.

Now it is your turn to write an ABAB poem. Here are a few rhyming words that you can use if you want to. Just make sure you write your poem in the ABAB pattern. (**Hint:** Don't write A or B in front of your lines. I just put them there so you could see the pattern.)

shower : flower   sow : grow   play : stay   aim : game

eat : seat   late : plate   rain : pane   sun : fun

_____

_____

_____

_____

1st Quarter Review (Each question is 5 points) Students may use the study sheets in the back of the book.

Write a proper noun for each common noun.

(1) state _____

(2) city _____

Write the possessive form of each noun.

(3) boy _____

(4) cat _____

Study the sentences:

I am going to a new class.
We are going to a new class.

(5) What is the singular pronoun in the first sentence? _____

(6) What is the plural pronoun in the second sentence? _____

Study the sentence:

Claire and I are going to a new class.
We are going to a new class.

(7) What are the antecedents? _____

Study the sentence:

It is my class.

(8) What is the possessive pronoun? _____

(9) What belongs to the possessive pronoun? _____

Study the sentence:

An owl and bat came to see the chicks.

(10) What is the subject of this sentence?

_____

(11) What conjunction was used in the compound subject?

_____

(12) Write a sentence using an action verb.

_____

Circle the helping verb and underline the main verb in each sentence.

(13) Micah does play with building blocks.

(14) Jin will help Micah.

(15) Micah and Jin should clean the room first.

(16) The boys might build a tent with their building blocks.

(17) The boys were building the tower quickly.

(18) Look at the previous five sentences. Find the state of being verb used as a helping verb. _____

Write **H** after the sentences that use a helping verb.

If it is a linking verb, write **L** after the sentences that use a linking verb. (**Hint:** Remember, helping verbs help the main verb in a sentence.)

(19) Micah is writing in his journal. _____

(20) Micah and Claire are best friends. _____

Flight Plan!

(21) Use your finger to trace the route to get the plane to the airport. Then use a marker to mark the path.

1st Quarter Review (Each question is 4 points) Students may use the study sheets in the back of the book.

Correctly match the four types of sentences:

(1) Imperative

(2) Declarative

(3) Exclamatory

(4) Interrogative

Asks a question

Expresses strong emotion

Makes a statement

Gives a command

Underline the subject and circle the predicate of each sentence.

(5) Micah jumped into the car.

(6) Alexia smiled at him.

(7) Combine the two sentences into one.

Micah went for a walk with Jin.
Micah went for a walk with Claire.

_____

_____

(8) Write a sentence using an interjection.

_____

_____

Name the conjunctions the acronym **fanboys** stands for.

(9) F _____   (12) B _____

(10) A _____   (13) O _____

(11) N _____   (14) Y _____

(15) S _____

Add quotation marks to the sentence.

(16) Claire asked Did you show Jin the Temple?

Put commas where they go in the sentences.

(17) Does Claire know about the Temple Micah?

(18) Claire did you see the Temple?

(19) How long Mr. Cunningham did it take to build?

Underline the titles in the sentences below.

(20) Dinosaurs by Design has a lot of good information.

(21) I was in a play called The Christmas Story.

(22) Have you watched A Jurassic Ark Mystery by Buddy Davis?

Write the names of the book, movie, or play correctly.

(23) swamp man! _____

(24) life in the great ice age _____

(25) Write a paragraph about your favorite person in the Bible. Check off each part as you write your paragraph:

○ Write the topic sentence. Remember to indent your topic sentence.

○ Write 2–3 sentences that give details about your topic. (**Hint:** Include reasons why he or she is your favorite and what this person did that you liked or didn't like.)

○ Write a concluding sentence.

_____

_____

_____

_____

_____

_____

Did you use a capital letter to start each sentence? Did you use correct punctuation at the end of each sentence? Good job!

READING COMPREHENSION

Read "Elijah" on pages 98–99 of *101 Favorite Stories from the Bible* with your teacher.

Answer the questions on page 99.

Copy Psalm 33:18–19, then memorize it with your teacher.

_____

_____

_____

_____

Copy the picture on page 99. Color your picture.

Copy the caption from page 99.

_____

_____

_____

_____

_____

_____

Spelling Review

Use your flashcards to practice your spelling words.

You may:

- Ask someone to quiz you on how to spell the words
- Play spelling games found in the back of the book
- Create your own spelling games
- Use each word in a sentence and say it to your teacher

 CREATE YOUR OWN DICTIONARY!

Students may choose their own words this week for their dictionary.

Fig Cakes

At the church Thanksgiving dinner, Micah told Claire he had been thinking about their last Sunday school lesson. "Mr. C. could have been talking about me because I wanted to stay behind in the other class. I didn't want to move, but now I see how important it is to seek God first and trust him enough to take the next step. I hope I never forget that like King Solomon did."

"That's great, Micah. Maybe you could build your own LEGO® temple to help you remember!" said Claire.

"Wow, that's a FANTASTIC idea!" Micah said. "I'm sure Jin will want to help, and I bet Mr. C. will even give us some tips for getting started!"

When it was time for dessert, Claire offered Micah one of the special treats she brought. "I asked my mom to help me find a recipe for something they might have eaten at a celebration in ancient Israel, and this is what we found — fig cakes. I made them myself!" Micah hesitated. His heart and belly were set on pumpkin pie, but Claire persisted. "Trust me, Micah, they are really good. They taste like Fig Newtons, only better!" Micah took a small bite and had to agree. Gobbling down the rest of his piece and reaching for another, he realized he was getting good at trying new things!

Later that night, Claire thought about what Micah said and wondered if there were areas in her own life where she needed to trust God more.

NARRATION PRACTICE

(1) Where does the story take place?

(2) What did Micah and Claire talk about at the beginning of the story?

(3) What idea did Claire have?

(4) What dessert did Claire offer to Micah?

(5) What did Micah notice about himself?

(6) What did Claire wonder about?

Picture Map

Sometimes you will find a map that uses only pictures to give you important information. Look at the map for a moment. See if you can complete the following directions:

- Using a red marker, circle the fountain.

- Using a green marker, circle the park bench.

- Using an orange marker, draw a rectangle around the building with stairs on the outside.

- Using a blue marker, circle the person mailing a letter.

Now, see what other details you can discover from the map. Discuss and explain your answers to these questions.

(1) Is it a sunny or rainy day?

(2) Do people in this town like to use cars or bikes?

(3) How many bike racks can you see?

(4) How many buildings do you see?

(5) How many round or rounded windows can you find?

INDEPENDENT READING

Verb Tense

A verb can tell us whether the sentence takes place in the past, present, or future. We call this **verb tense**.

Let's see how we can use the verb *run* to show action in the past, present, and future. (**Hint:** The future tense uses the helping verb *will* or *shall*.)

I ran fast. (Past)
I run fast. (Present)
I will run fast. (Future)

Write past, present, or future next to each sentence.

(1) Claire will bake fig cakes. _____

(2) Claire gave Micah a fig cake. _____

(3) Micah eats the fig cake. _____

Sometimes we can add the suffix -ed or -d to a verb to show it happened in the past. Study the example:

Claire called Micah over to her table.

(4) What word was the suffix -ed added to? _____

Jin lived in another state.

(5) What word was the suffix -d added to? _____

Sometimes we can add the suffix -ing to a verb to show it is happening in the present. (**Hint:** Sometimes when -ing is added to a verb, the present tense uses a helping verb before the main verb.

Study the example:

Micah is eating a fig cake.

(6) What word was the suffix -ing added to? _____

Use the verb to write a sentence in the past, present, and future. (**Hint:** You may need to change the verb. You may also need to use a helping verb.)

cook

Past:

_____

_____

Present:

_____

_____

Future:

_____

_____

Dictionary Guide Words

 **TEACHER NOTE** • The student will need a dictionary for this lesson. A children's dictionary is recommended.

Ask your teacher for a dictionary. Open the dictionary to any page. You will see two words at the top of the page, usually one on each side. These are called **guide words**. They tell you the first and last words that are found on the page.

Here is an example of guide words:

mesh	might

Now, look at the words with definitions listed on the page of your dictionary. They are in alphabetical order. The first word is the first guide word. The last word is the last guide word.

In our example of the guide words *mesh* and *might*, words listed on the page in alphabetical order could include: **mess, method, mice, middle**. These words are in alphabetical order. They are after *mesh* but before *might*.

Guide words make it easier to look up words in the dictionary.

Open your dictionary to any page. Write the guide words:

_____   _____

Write any four words found on the page in alphabetical order:

_____

_____

_____

_____

Put the following words under the correct guide words:

huge   house   hope   hornet   hoot   howl

hook	horse

hour	human

(1) _____   (4) _____

(2) _____   (5) _____

(3) _____   (6) _____

A dictionary can show us how to say a word. Look up the word *chase* in your dictionary. Right after the word, you are shown how to say the word. The phonics markings show how to say the vowel. My dictionary shows it like this:

chase (chās)

Look up these words in your dictionary. How fast can you find them? Copy how to say each word.

(7) cheap _____

(8) scale _____

(9) nail _____

(10) broke _____

(II) Micah and Claire spoke of building a temple from LEGOs® as a reminder of what King Solomon did. There was a plan for the temple and it would help Micah if he could understand the plan. Look at the empty shape below. Now, look at the four images below it. Which one of the four images could create the shape we see? This may be a little difficult, so take your time. Imagine the pieces fitting together in different ways to fill the shape.

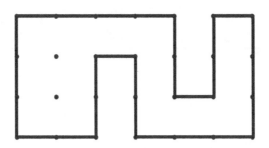

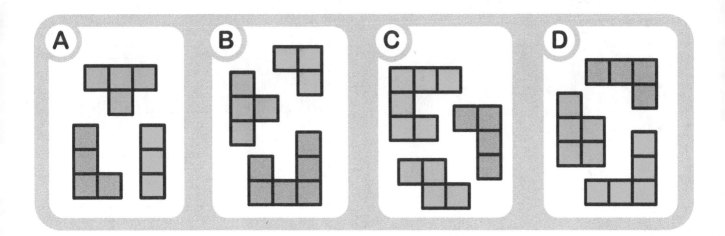

Read "The Lord God or Baal?" on pages 100–101 of *101 Favorite Stories from the Bible* with your teacher.

Answer the questions on page 101.

Copy Matthew 4:10b, then memorize it with your teacher.

_____

_____

_____

_____

Copy the picture on page 101. Color your picture.

Copy the caption from page 101.

_____

_____

_____

_____

_____

_____

Compound Words

Compound words are two words made into one to create a new meaning.

 Some compound words need a hyphen between them.

 Open compounds need a space between the two words.

Learn to spell these words:

> bedroom, fingernail, fireplace, get-together,
> homesick, ice cream, newspaper, pinecone, railroad,
> seat belt, sunflower, tailgate, twenty-one, wheelchair,

Use the picture clues to create compound words.

(1) _____

(2) _____

(3) _____

(4) _____

(5) _____

(6) _____

(7) _____

(8) _____

(9) _____

(10)_____

Write the compound spelling words that use a hyphen.

(11) _____   (12) _____

Write the open compound spelling words. Remember to add a space between the words.

(13) _____   (14) _____

Write a fun sentence using at least two of your spelling words.

_____

_____

Be sure to start each sentence with a capital letter and end it with a punctuation mark.

For More Practice:

Write your words in the shape boxes using the worksheet for this lesson available as a free download at masterbooks.com/classroom-aids.

Write your spelling words on notecards. Write one word on each card. You may create right-brain flashcards with your words.

Ask your teacher to read each spelling word. Spell the word out loud and use it in a sentence.

 CREATE YOUR OWN DICTIONARY!

Title: The Lost Piece of Silver

Artist: James Tissot

Scripture Connection

Ask your teacher to read to you Luke 15:8–10 from your Bible.

 **OBSERVATION SKILLS**

(1) Who is in the picture?

(2) What is happening in the picture?

(3) What colors are used in the picture?

(4) How does this picture make you feel? Why?

(5) What can we learn from this picture and the story it tells?

Story Writing

Finish the story using at least three sentences.

The family packed up their van for a trip. Everyone buckled up their seat belts and got ready for a long ride. They turned out of their driveway and started down the road. They only drove for about ten minutes when they had to pull over. They had a flat tire!

_____

_____

_____

_____

_____

_____

_____

INDEPENDENT READING

 **GRAMMAR PRACTICE**

Verb Phrase

Do you remember our helping verbs? Remember, state of being verbs can be helping verbs.

State of Being Verbs

| is | am | are | was | were | be | been | being |

Helping Verbs

has	have	had		do	does	did
can	will	shall		could	would	should
must	may	might				

A **phrase** is a small group of words. A **helping verb phrase** is a small group of helping verbs. There are many helping verb phrases. Some examples include:

| can be | could be | may be | might be |
| has been | have been | had been | might have been |

Here is a helping verb phrase used in a sentence:

> Micah could be eating a fig cake.

(1) What is the helping verb phrase used in the sentence?

_____

A **verb phrase** is a helping verb (or helping verb phrase) and the main verb. Look at the sentence again.

(2) What is the verb phrase? _____

Write a sentence using a verb phrase.

_____

_____

What helping verbs did you use? _____

What main verb did you use?_____

Fig Facts!

Micah loved the fig cakes! Figs are from trees that are native to the Middle East. Countries like Turkey and Egypt produce the bulk of fig crops. Figs are in season from around August to October. You can find fresh figs in grocery stores sometimes, but most of the time they are dried because of the difficulty in transporting them for sale in stores.

We create a contraction when we take two words and make them into one by removing some letters. We use an apostrophe where we removed letters. Study the example:

$$are + not = aren't$$

Match the contractions to the words:

(1) can't   here is   (5) I'm   we would

(2) don't   do not   (6) she'll   I am

(3) he's   can not   (7) they're   she will

(4) here's   he is   (8) we'd   they are

Write the correct contractions:

(9) are not _____   (13) must not _____

(10) does not _____   (14) she has _____

(11) he would _____   (15) there is _____

(12) I have _____   (16) will not _____

Write the two words used for the contractions:

(17) didn't _____   (21) wasn't _____

(18) it's _____   (22) we're _____

(19) she'd _____   (23) who'll _____

(20) they've _____   (24) you're _____

READING COMPREHENSION

Read "Elijah Goes to Heaven" on pages 102–103 of *101 Favorite Stories from the Bible* with your teacher.

Answer the questions on page 103.

Copy 2 Timothy 4:7–8a, then memorize it with your teacher.

_____

_____

_____

_____

Copy the picture on page 103. Color your picture.

Copy the caption from page 103.

_____

_____

_____

_____

_____

_____

 **SPELLING PRACTICE**

Contractions

We are going to work with contractions.

Contractions are two words that are shortened into one, with an apostrophe in place of the missing letters.

Learn to spell these words:

> can't, could've, didn't, don't, haven't, I'd, I'm, I've,
> it's, shouldn't, wasn't, won't, would've, you'd

Write the correct contractions in the story.

(1) _____ about four hours before I leave on my trip.

(2) I _____ packed earlier, but I _____ have time.

(3) I _____ find one pair of matching socks!

(4) I _____ have waited so long to pack.

(5) I _____ checked the dryer yet. I hope they are in there!

(6) I _____ checked sooner if I _____ so busy.

(7) _____ waited too long to find my socks.

(8) I _____ know what _____ going to do!

(9) _____ think _____ own at least one pair of matching socks!

(10) It looks like I _____ be wearing socks on my trip!

Write a fun sentence using at least two contractions from your spelling words that use the word *not*.

_____

_____

Write a fun sentence using at least one contraction from your spelling words that use the word *have*.

_____

_____

Be sure to start each sentence with a capital letter and end it with a punctuation mark.

For More Practice:

Write your words in the shape boxes using the worksheet for this lesson available as a free download at masterbooks.com/classroom-aids.

Write your spelling words on notecards. Write one word on each card. You may create right-brain flashcards with your words.

Ask your teacher to read each spelling word. Spell the word out loud and use it in a sentence.

CREATE YOUR OWN DICTIONARY!

The Christmas Play

Claire was excited as she and Ava walked into the auditorium. They had just learned that Mrs. Pruitt was about to announce the title of this year's Christmas play.

As she walked onto the stage, Mrs. Pruitt motioned for everyone to quiet down. "I'm very happy to see that so many are interested in the play this year. We have been looking through various scripts for the past several weeks and have finally decided on a play called *A Brand New Star*. There will be three main characters and lots of supporting roles in addition to opportunities to work backstage. Of course, everyone will be part of the choir. I will be choosing the parts in the next few days and will announce them at our first practice."

Claire could not contain her enthusiasm. This was one of her favorite activities! She had always had a main part in past performances and usually got assigned to sing a solo as well. Remembering how nervous she was that first year, Claire was thankful she had the confidence that came with experience now. How she loved performing!

Ava was just the opposite. "I bet you get one of the lead parts, Claire," she said. "I sure hope I don't get a speaking part. I would much rather be part of the chorus or maybe even help behind the scenes. Maybe Mrs. Pruitt will let me help design costumes or props."

Both girls left the auditorium with their own idea of how things would turn out.

NARRATION PRACTICE

(1) Why was Claire excited?

(2) What announcements did Mrs. Pruitt make?

(3) Why did Ava not want a speaking part?

(4) What did Ava say about Mrs. Pruitt's announcements?

Acronyms

An **acronym** is a special kind of abbreviation. Abbreviate means to shorten. An acronym shortens a word usually by using the first letter of each word. Acronyms are different from abbreviations because they make a new word. Are you ready to see an example?

The acronym for *self-contained underwater breathing apparatus* is scuba.

Do you see the acronym?

Self-Contained Underwater Breathing Apparatus

Can you think of a reason why divers may want to use the acronym *scuba* whenever they ask a friend to go diving with them? "Hey, Dylan, do you want to go self-contained underwater breathing apparatus diving with me today?"

Now it's your turn. Write the acronym.

(1) **National Aeronautics and Space Administration** _____

Now for the fun part. Usually, acronyms are created because people don't want to say a whole phrase every time they talk about something, like in our example of scuba diving.

We are going to do something different. Let's make acronyms a fun way! Let's take regular words and see if we can make them stand for a phrase. Here is an example:

L-love
A-always
U-understands
G-giggles
H-happily

You give it a try. Use a blank piece of paper and write a word down the page. Make your own acronym.

Verb Agreement

When we write a sentence, the subject and the linking verb must agree. This is a fancy way of saying we need to use the correct linking verb with our subject.

Remember, the subject tells who or what our sentence is about. A linking verb links a noun or adjective to the subject of the sentence.

How do we make sure our subject and linking verb agree?

- First, we look at our subject. Is it singular or plural? (**Hint:** Singular means one. Plural means more than one.)

- Then we look at our linking verb. Is it present or past tense?

- Check the chart to make sure we used the right linking verb for our subject.

Let's study the chart:

Verb Agreement		
Subject	Present Tense	Past Tense
Singular: he, she, it	is	was
Plural: we, they, you	are	were
I	am	was

Draw a line to the correct linking verb for each sentence. (**Hint:** We have used pronouns in our chart. We have not used pronouns in our sentences. Ask yourself what pronoun could have been used for the subject.)

(1) Claire and Ava _____ at church. (present)   are

(2) Claire and Ava _____ at church. (past)   were

(3) Claire _____ excited. (past)   is

(4) Claire _____ excited. (present)   was

(5) I _____ hoping to get a solo in the play. (past)   am

(6) I _____ hoping to get a solo in the play. (present)   was

Write a sentence using a singular subject and a present tense linking verb.

_____

_____

Write a sentence using a plural subject and a past tense linking verb.

_____

_____

Write a sentence using the word *I* as the subject and a past tense linking verb.

_____

_____

 **JUST 4 FUN!**

All About Acronyms!

Acronyms are a form of writing where the first letters of a phrase are used to tell you something. For example:

Laugh Out Loud!   Its acronym is LOL!

Look at the list of acronyms below. See if you can match them with the phrase they represent. When you get finished, look around your house or room and see what acronyms you can find!

(7) AC   Peanut Butter and Jelly

(8) PBJ   Air Conditioning

(9) Q&A   As Soon As Possible

(10) TLC   Question and Answer

(11) VIP   Very Important Person

(12) ASAP   Tender Loving Care

Abbreviations

Abbreviate means to shorten. Do you remember how to abbreviate the days of the weeks and the months of the year? If you need some extra practice, use the practice pages in the back of the book.

We can abbreviate the names of states in two ways. We abbreviate state names one way when we write a sentence. We end this type of abbreviation with a period.

We abbreviate state names another way for an address. We use two capital letters, and we do not add a period when we abbreviate for a postal address.

Draw a line from each state to the correct abbreviation. The regular abbreviation and Post Office abbreviation is given. The states that begin with the same letter can be tricky so study them closely! (**Hint:** Some states only have a postal abbreviation.)

State	Post Office	Abbreviation
(1) Alabama	CA	Calif.
(2) Alaska	AR	Ark.
(3) Arizona	AL	Ala.
(4) Arkansas	AK	
(5) California	AZ	Ariz.
(6) Colorado	GA	Ga.
(7) Connecticut	DE	Del.
(8) Delaware	CT	Conn.
(9) Florida	CO	Colo.
(10) Georgia	FL	Fla.
(11) Hawaii	ID	
(12) Idaho	IA	
(13) Illinois	IN	Ind.
(14) Indiana	IL	Ill.
(15) Iowa	HI	

State	Post Office	Abbreviation
(16) Kansas	ME	Me.
(17) Kentucky	MD	Md.
(18) Louisiana	KY	Ky.
(19) Maine	LA	La.
(20) Maryland	KS	Kan.
(21) Massachusetts	MI	Mich.
(22) Michigan	MA	Mass.
(23) Minnesota	MS	Miss.
(24) Mississippi	MO	Mo.
(25) Missouri	MN	Minn.
(26) Montana	NJ	N.J.
(27) Nebraska	MT	Mont.
(28) Nevada	NH	N.H.
(29) New Hampshire	NE	Neb.
(30) New Jersey	NV	Nev.
(31) New Mexico	NC	N.C.
(32) New York	ND	N.D.
(33) North Carolina	OH	
(34) North Dakota	NY	N.Y.
(35) Ohio	NM	N.M.

State	Post Office	Abbreviation
(36) Oklahoma	OR	Or.
(37) Oregon	OK	Okla.
(38) Pennsylvania	PA	Pa.
(39) Rhode Island	SC	S.C.
(40) South Carolina	RI	R.I.
(41) South Dakota	VT	Vt.
(42) Tennessee	TX	Tex.
(43) Texas	TN	Tenn.
(44) Utah	SD	S.D.
(45) Vermont	UT	
(46) Virginia	WI	Wis.
(47) Washington	WV	W. Va.
(48) West Virginia	VA	Va.
(49) Wisconsin	WY	Wyo.
(50) Wyoming	WA	Wash.

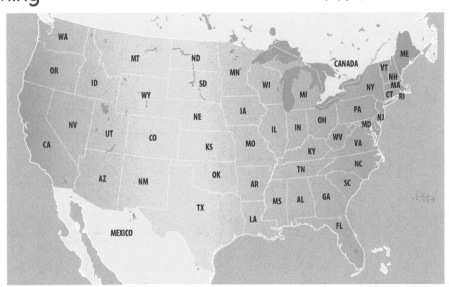

READING COMPREHENSION

Read "Naaman is Healed" on pages 104–105 of *101 Favorite Stories from the Bible* with your teacher.

Answer the questions on page 105.

Copy Luke 5:13, then memorize it with your teacher.

_____

_____

_____

_____

Copy the picture on page 105. Color your picture.

Copy the caption from page 105.

_____

_____

_____

_____

_____

_____

**SPELLING PRACTICE**

Plural Words

We are going to work with plural words. Plural means more than one.

We make many words plural by adding -s.

When a word ends in a vowel and *y*, add -s.

When a word ends in a vowel and *o*, add -s.

When a word ends in *s, ss, sh, ch, z*, or *x*, add -es.

When a word ends with a consonant and *o*, add -es.

Watch out for these rule breakers:

| piano = pianos | photo = photos |

Learn to spell these words:

> boxes, buses, chimneys, churches, fleas, foxes, fusses,
> heroes, photos, pianos, rocks, rodeos, themes, wishes

Write a fun sentence using at least two of your spelling words that end in *s*.

_____

_____

Write a fun sentence using at least two of your spelling words that end in *es*.

_____

_____

Be sure to start your sentence with a capital letter and end it with a punctuation mark.

Create your own word search using the spelling words. Follow the example.

- boxes
- buses
- chimneys
- churches
- fleas
- foxes
- fusses
- heroes
- photos
- pianos
- rocks
- rodeos
- themes
- wishes

For More Practice:

Write your words in the shape boxes using the worksheet for this lesson available as a free download at masterbooks.com/classroom-aids.

Write your spelling words on notecards. Write one word on each card. You may create right-brain flashcards with your words.

Ask your teacher to read each spelling word. Spell the word out loud and use it in a sentence.

CREATE YOUR OWN DICTIONARY!

Trees

By Sara Coleridge

The Oak is called the king of trees,
The Aspen quivers in the breeze,
The Poplar grows up straight and tall,
The Peach tree spreads along the wall,
The Sycamore gives pleasant shade,
The Willow droops in watery glade,
The Fir tree useful in timber gives,
The Beech amid the forest lives.

Comprehension

Were there any words you didn't understand? Circle them.

TEACHER NOTE

- The teacher should go over with the student the meaning of the circled words in the context of the poem.

NARRATION PRACTICE

(1) What is the title of the poem?

(2) What is this poem about?

(3) Think about each kind of tree. Can you explain why the poem's author describes each tree like she does?

(4) Why do you think the author wrote this poem?

(5) Explain how this poem makes you feel.

TEACHER NOTE

- The teacher may want to help the student research each type of tree. Students may want to compare the trees with the poem's description. Students may want to draw a picture of each tree, showing how the poem's author describes it.

Coleridge, Sara. (1853) *Pretty Lessons in Verse, for Good Children; with Some Lessons in Latin in Easy Rhyme*. London: J.W. Parker & Son., p. 15.

Memorization

Memorize the poem with your teacher.

Rhyming

Write two sentences that end in words that rhyme. (**Hint:** Study the poem you read to see how each line rhymes with the next.)

_____

_____

Write two more sentences that end in words that rhyme.

_____

_____

INDEPENDENT READING

GRAMMAR PRACTICE

See – Saw – Seen;
Real – Really

We are going to work with some more verbs: **see, saw, seen**.

I see.	I saw.	I have seen.

The verbs *see* and *saw* are used alone.

The verb *see* refers to the present.

The verb *saw* refers to the past.

The verb *seen* refers to the past and needs a helping verb.

Study the examples:

I see Mrs. Pruitt on the stage.
I saw Claire in her seat.
I have seen Ava in the room.

Fill in the blank with the correct verb: **see   saw   seen**

(1) I have _____ the script of the play.

(2) Mrs. Pruitt _____ Claire.

(3) I _____ Ava and Claire.

Draw a line from the verb to the correct description. (**Hint:** Some verbs have more than one description.)

(4) **see**   refers to the past

(5) **saw**   refers to the present

(6) **seen**   used alone

                          needs a helping verb

Write a sentence using **see**.

_____

Write a sentence using **saw**.

_____

Write a sentence using **seen**.

_____

Do you ever wonder when to use the word _real_ and when to use the word _really_? It helps to know the definition of a word.

Real means it exists. It is not pretend or made up.

Really means very.

Study the examples:

> Jin hoped they could use a real donkey for the play.
> Micah was really happy to run the sound board.

Now it is your turn. Write the correct word in the sentences: **real or really**

(7) Jin was _____ surprised he got a lead part in the play.

(8) A _____ camel would be fun in the play.

(9) Claire was _____ upset she didn't get a lead role in the play.

(10) Ava was _____ sad for Claire.

(11) Ava knew she wasn't a _____ actor.

Abbreviations

We may use initials to abbreviate the first, middle, or last name of a person.

Example: The abbreviation for Abraham Lincoln is A. L.

Write your teacher's initials. _____

When a son has the same name as his father, we call him a *junior*. We can abbreviate Junior with Jr. We call the dad *senior*. We can abbreviate Senior with Sr. Use a capital letter when abbreviating titles. Study the examples:

John Jr. helped his dad cut down the fir tree.
John Sr. was thankful for the help.

Write a sentence using the abbreviation for Junior.

_____

Write a sentence using the abbreviation for Senior.

_____

Do you remember how to abbreviate the titles of people? You may look in the back of the book if you need to study them.

Match the titles to the correct abbreviations.

(1) Mister   Mrs.   (8) Captain   Gen.

(2) Miss   Mr.   (9) General   Sgt.

(3) Missus   Ms.   (10) Sergeant   Capt.

(4) Doctor   Det.   (11) Honorable   Sen.

(5) Reverend   Prof.   (12) Senator   Hon.

(6) Detective   Dr.   (13) Representative   Pres.

(7) Professor   Rev.   (14) President   Rep.

Did you know there are lots of names for streets? Many times they are abbreviated. Copy the names used for streets and their abbreviations.

Avenue = Ave. _____

Drive = Dr. _____

Lane = Ln. _____

Road = Rd. _____

Route = Rt. _____

Street = St. _____

There are even more names for streets! Can you figure out the abbreviation for each one? Draw a line from the name of each street to the correct abbreviation:

(15) Boulevard   Pl.

(16) Court   Terr.

(17) Highway   Ct.

(18) Parkway   Blvd.

(19) Place   Tpke.

(20) Terrace   Hwy.

(21) Turnpike   Pkwy.

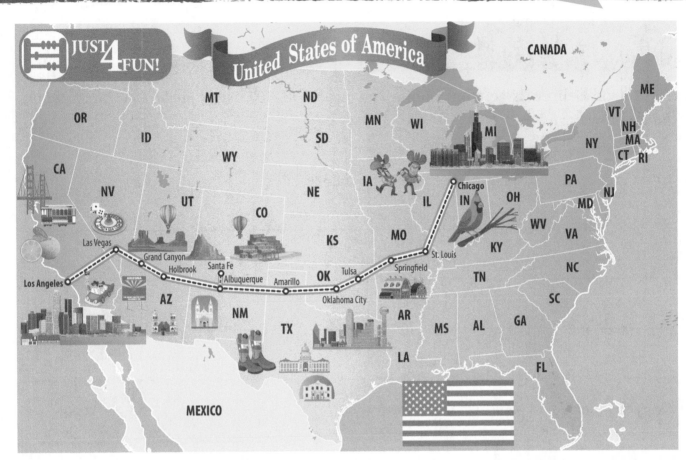

After cars were invented, people were able to travel long distances much faster and easier than before. Because of this, highways were built to make it even easier to travel from one place in the United States to another. One of the first highways, and most famous, is Route 66, which went across half of the country. Write out the names below for the eight states that it crosses:

(1) _____   (5) _____

(2) _____   (6) _____

(3) _____   (7) _____

(4) _____   (8) _____

(9) What two cities were at the beginning and end of Route 66?

_____

READING COMPREHENSION

Read "God Delivers Israel from Famine" on pages 106–107 of *101 Favorite Stories from the Bible* with your teacher.

Answer the questions on page 107.

Copy Proverbs 28:1, then memorize it with your teacher.

_____

_____

_____

_____

Copy the picture on page 107. Color your picture.

Copy the caption from page 107.

_____

_____

_____

_____

_____

_____

_____

 **SPELLING PRACTICE**

More Plural Words

When a word ends in the letter *f* or *fe*, we make it plural by changing the *f* or *fe* to *v* and then add -es.

Watch out for these rule breakers:

roof = roofs	cliff = cliffs

When a word ends in a consonant and the letter *y*, we make it plural by changing the *y* to *i* and then add -es.

Learn to spell these words:

> calves, cliffs, countries, enemies, halves, ladies, leaves,
> lives, mysteries, roofs, supplies, twenties, wives, wolves

Write the plural form of each word.

(1) leaf _____

(2) wolf _____

(3) wife _____

(4) calf _____

(5) life _____

(6) half _____

(7) enemy _____

(8) country _____

(9) supply _____

(10) mystery _____

(11) twenty _____

(12) lady _____

(13) roof _____

(14) cliff _____

Write a fun sentence using at least two of your spelling words that end in *-ves*.

_____

_____

Write a fun sentence using at least two of your spelling words that end in *-ies*.

_____

_____

Write a fun sentence using the two spelling words that break the rules.

_____

_____

Be sure to start each sentence with a capital letter and end it with a punctuation mark.

For More Practice:

Write your words in the shape boxes using the worksheet for this lesson available as a free download at masterbooks.com/classroom-aids.

Write your spelling words on notecards. Write one word on each card. You may create right-brain flashcards with your words.

Ask your teacher to read each spelling word. Spell the word out loud and use it in a sentence.

 CREATE YOUR OWN DICTIONARY!

Play Practice

Excitement was in the air as Claire, Ava, Micah, and Jin talked in the hallway before practice.

"I'm pretty sure I'll be helping with sound again this year," Micah said.

"You are the only kid who knows anything about the sound system, so you are probably right. I'm not much of an actor, so I'll probably be a donkey or a camel," Jin said jokingly. Micah laughed and chimed in, "You do have a mean *hee-haw*!"

Claire grabbed Ava's hand and said, "Here comes Mrs. Pruitt. Lets go grab a seat."

You could have heard a pin drop as she made her way to the stage. "After much prayer and consideration, we have selected parts for our play. The three lead characters will be played by Jin, Alexia, and Ava." Claire's heart sank. As Mrs. Pruitt began to list who would have the supporting roles, it soon became apparent she was not on that list either! She was happy to hear that Micah was assigned to the sound board. Everyone else would be part of the chorus, and all cast members would be expected to help with costumes, props, and scene changes.

Her tears fell freely as Claire got ready for bed. It felt good to let them out after blinking them back through the entire practice. As she listened to Mrs. Pruitt talk about working together for a common goal, she tried to feel excited for the play, and for Ava. She just couldn't. Ava didn't even want a lead part. It seemed so unfair.

NARRATION PRACTICE

(1) Why did Jin think Micah would be picked to run sound for the play?

(2) Why did Jin think he would probably be a donkey or a camel?

(3) Who was given the parts of the three lead characters?

(4) What would everyone else do?

(5) Why was Claire upset?

Writing a Story

Write a short story about the picture using at least three or four sentences. Be sure to describe the dog in your story.

_____

_____

_____

_____

_____

_____

GRAMMAR PRACTICE

Eat – Ate – Eaten; Go – Went – Gone

We are going to work with some more verbs: *eat, ate, eaten* and *go, went, gone.*

Present	Past	Past–Helping Verb
I eat.	I ate.	I have eaten.
I go.	I went.	I have gone.

The verbs *eat* and *go* refer to the present.

> I eat a snack under the tree.
> I go climb a tree every day.

The verbs *ate* and *went* refer to the past.

> I ate lunch under an oak tree.
> I went to see the peach tree.

The verbs *eaten* and *gone* refer to the past and need a helping verb.

> I have eaten peaches from the tree.
> I have gone to pick acorns.

Draw a line from each verb to the correct place in time.

(1) **gone**   present

(2) **go**   past

(3) **went**   past with helping verb

(4) **eaten**   present

(5) **ate**   past

(6) **eat**   past with helping verb

Draw a line from the sentence to the correct verb:

(7) I have _____ lunch already.   eat

(8) I _____ my last peach earlier.   eaten

(9) I _____ peaches every day.   ate

Write a sentence using **go.**

_____

_____

Write a sentence using **went.**

_____

_____

Write a sentence using **gone.**

_____

_____

Tell your teacher a story using the words e*at, ate,* and *eaten.* Be sure to use complete sentences when telling your story.

Synonyms, Antonyms, Thesaurus

> Synonyms are two words that mean the same thing.

> Antonyms are two words that have opposite meanings.

Here are some examples of synonyms:

fearful : afraid   leave : exit   sloppy : messy

Here are some examples of antonyms:

fearful : brave   leave : arrive   sloppy : neat

Write a synonym and antonym for each word:

frown: _____   _____

moist: _____   _____

pause: _____   _____

rich: _____   _____

A **thesaurus** is a book of synonyms and antonyms. We can use a thesaurus to help us find the best words to use in our writing.

Do you remember how to look up words in a dictionary? Finding words in the thesaurus is done the same way. Instead of giving you the definition of a word, a thesaurus gives you synonyms and antonyms of a word.

Ask your teacher for a thesaurus. Find in the thesaurus the word: **blossom**

Write a synonym and an antonym for the word **blossom**.

_____   _____

Write a sentence using a synonym for the word **blossom**.

_____

_____

Write a sentence using an antonym for the word **blossom**.

_____

_____

It's Christmas! Time to plug in the Christmas tree. Can you follow the cord from the star on top to the bottom of the tree? Use a dark marker or pen and trace the right path for the cord.

READING COMPREHENSION

Read "Jehoshaphat's Singing Army" on pages 108–109 of *101 Favorite Stories from the Bible* with your teacher.

Answer the questions on page 109.

Copy Psalm 107:1, then memorize it with your teacher.

_____

_____

_____

_____

Copy the picture on page 109. Color your picture.

Copy the caption from page 109.

_____

_____

_____

_____

_____

_____

SPELLING PRACTICE

Irregular Plural Words

We are going to work with irregular plural words.

Learn to spell these words:

> cacti, children, corn, deer, fish, geese, mice,
> moose, octopi, oxen, people, seaweed, sheep, women

Find the spelling words in the word search.

- ○ cacti
- ○ children
- ○ corn
- ○ deer
- ○ fish
- ○ geese
- ○ mice
- ○ moose
- ○ octopi
- ○ oxen
- ○ people
- ○ seaweed
- ○ sheep
- ○ women

```
X H S O U G B J N E N U F N C
R Q S U O K A O C T O P I K S
E K C W X S R I L N O D H U C
L Q N O N Z M T E Z E T H B C
P U P Y R S G X F E C I P L H
C S X O O N O A W V H K F R O
O O C A C T I A Y S I O P F E
W P E O G F E O A W L I H R Q
B E A N E S I G E G D A P K U
V O N V E E I S A N R L X X X
L P O O S E N S H E E P D N Z
F L L P E E D T O S N B E P B
Y E O Z M C H F R C H L E Y D
A I V O Z U Z I H Y E F R X S
Z K W G K K N A X W M O O S E
```

TEACHER NOTE
- You may explain to the student that it is also correct to say "octopuses."

Write a fun sentence using at least two of your spelling words.

_____

_____

Write a fun sentence using at least two more of your spelling words.

_____

_____

Be sure to start each sentence with a capital letter and end it with a punctuation mark.

For More Practice:

Write your words in the shape boxes using the worksheet for this lesson available as a free download at masterbooks.com/classroom-aids.

Write your spelling words on notecards. Write one word on each card. You may create right-brain flashcards with your words.

Ask your teacher to read each spelling word. Spell the word out loud and use it in a sentence.

 CREATE YOUR OWN DICTIONARY!

Title: The Net

Artist: Anna Belle Lee Washington

 **OBSERVATION SKILLS**

(1) In what season do you think this painting takes place?

(2) What is happening in this painting?

(3) What things do you see in the picture?

(4) Describe the people in this painting.

(5) What colors are used in this picture?

(6) How does this picture make you feel? Why?

Story Writing

Finish this story about the picture. Use at least three sentences.

It was a Sunday afternoon. As the family left church, they were happy to see the sun was still shining. They had packed a lunch and wanted to eat it somewhere special. They couldn't agree where to eat so they took a vote.

_____

_____

_____

_____

_____

_____

_____

This – That – These – Those

We use the words *this* and *that* when we are talking about one of something. Remember, one of something is singular.

We use the word *this* if the object is close to the person speaking.

We use the word *that* if the object is far away.

We use the words *these* and *those* when we are talking about more than one of something. Remember, more than one of something is plural.

We use the word *these* if the object is close to the person speaking.

We use the word *those* if the object is far away.

	Near	Far
Singular	this	that
Plural	these	those

Match with the correct word to use:

(1) Singular, far   this   (3) Plural, near   these

(2) Singular, near   that   (4) Plural, far   those

Write a sentence using **this**.

_____

_____

Write a sentence using **those**.

_____

_____

Comparison using -er and -est

We can compare two things by using the suffixes -er and -est.

Adding -er to a word shows that there is more of something than another. Here is an example:

Alexia is taller than Micah.

We added the suffix -er to the word *tall* to show Alexia has more height than Micah.

Adding -est to a word shows that there is the most of something. Here is an example:

Alexia is the tallest child in her family.

We added the suffix -est to the word *tall* to show Alexia has the most height in her family.

If a word ends in an *e*, we remove the *e* before we add the suffix -er or -est.

Here is an example:

My cat is braver than my dog.
My cat is the bravest animal on my street.

We dropped the e before we added -er and -est to the word *brave*.

If a word ends in *y*, we change the *y* to *i* before we add the suffix -er or -est.

Here is an example:

My dog is noisier than my cat.
My dog is the noisiest dog on the block.

We changed the *y* to *i* before adding -er and -est to the word *noisy*.

If a word has one syllable, one vowel, and ends in one consonant, we double the last consonant before we add the suffix -er or -est.

Here is an example:

Our weather is hotter in the summer.
It is hottest in July.

We doubled the consonant *t* before we added -er and -est to the word *hot*.

Add the suffix -er and -est to the following words:

(1) **nice:** _____   _____

(2) **tall:** _____   _____

(3) **tasty:** _____   _____

(4) **wet:** _____   _____

(5) **great:** _____   _____

(6) **red:** _____   _____

(7) **safe:** _____   _____

(8) **happy:** _____   _____

READING COMPREHENSION

Read "Esther the Jewess" on pages 110–111 of *101 Favorite Stories from the Bible* with your teacher.

Answer the questions on page 111.

Copy Proverbs 21:21, then memorize it with your teacher.

_____

_____

_____

_____

Copy the picture on page 111. Color your picture.

Copy the caption from page 111.

_____

_____

_____

_____

_____

_____

SPELLING PRACTICE

Suffixes -er and -est

We use the suffixes -er and -est to form adjectives that compare.

When the word ends in the letter *e*, drop the final *e* before adding -er or -est.

When the word ends in the letter *y*, change the *y* to *i* before adding -er or -est.

When the word contains a short vowel, double the final consonant before adding -er or -est.

Learn to spell these words:

> closer, closest, funnier, funniest, greater, greatest, hotter, hottest, larger, largest, redder, reddest, taller, tallest

Add -er and -est to each word.

(1) tall _____ _____

(2) great _____ _____

(3) hot _____ _____

(4) red _____ _____

(5) funny _____ _____

(6) large _____ _____

(7) close _____ _____

Write a fun sentence using one of your spelling words.

_____

_____

Write a fun sentence using one more of your spelling words.

_____

_____

Be sure to start each sentence with a capital letter and end it with a punctuation mark.

For More Practice:

Write your words in the shape boxes using the worksheet for this lesson available as a free download at masterbooks.com/classroom-aids.

Write your spelling words on notecards. Write one word on each card. You may create right-brain flashcards with your words.

Ask your teacher to read each spelling word. Spell the word out loud and use it in a sentence.

CREATE YOUR OWN DICTIONARY!

Let's Get Busy!

Mrs. Pruitt pulled Claire aside before the next practice. "I meant to talk to you about this last week, but it was such a busy evening I didn't get around to it. This production is going to be our biggest ever, and I am going to need an assistant. Since I will be spending most of my time working with the choir, I need someone to work with the actors, helping them with their lines, and someone to oversee prop design and costumes. This is a big job, and I'd like you to pray about being the assistant director. With your experience and leadership skills, you would be perfect!"

Claire was stunned. Over the past week, she had been praying about the play and her part in it. She kept remembering her conversation with Micah about trusting God and had been asking Him to help her do just that. As she learned to let go of her own disappointment, she came to realize how much it could help Ava's faith grow as she trusted the Lord to help her handle this role. She had decided to be Ava's biggest cheerleader and to accept her part in the chorus with gratitude. Besides, she loved to sing!

"I have been praying all week, Mrs. Pruitt," Claire said. "The Lord helped me see that I should accept whatever role you gave me with gratitude. I just never expected something this amazing! I accept!"

"I'm so happy to hear that," Mrs. Pruitt said. "Now let's get busy. We have lots to do!"

(1) Why did Mrs. Pruitt pull Claire aside before practice?

(2) What conversation did Claire remember?

(3) What did Claire learn?

(4) What did the Lord help Claire to see?

Word Categories

The nouns, verbs, and adjectives have gotten all mixed up! Put them under the correct column.

run cat sweet pretty ball tree yell fast jump

Nouns	**Verbs**	**Adjectives**
(1) _____	(4) _____	(7) _____
(2) _____	(5) _____	(8) _____
(3) _____	(6) _____	(9) _____

Short Story

Write a short story using the nouns, verbs, and adjectives above.

_____

_____

_____

_____

_____

_____

GRAMMAR PRACTICE

It's – Its, Who's – Whose

The word *it's* is a contraction. Do you remember what a contraction is? A contraction is two words that are shortened into one. The word *it's* is a contraction of *it is*. Here is an example:

It's time to practice the play.

The word **it's** is a contraction that means *it is*. Read the sentence again and see if you could say "It is" instead of "it's." This is an easy way to see if a contraction is being used. In the sentence above, you can replace "It's" with "it is" so we know it is a contraction and needs an apostrophe.

A possessive noun shows who or what owns or has something. We make a singular noun possessive by adding an apostrophe and "s." The word **its** means possession or belonging, but we don't use an apostrophe in this case. It is an exception to the rule. Here is an example:

The donkey loved its apple.

The word **its** shows that the apple belongs to the donkey. Notice we didn't use an apostrophe and "s" to show possession. Only the contraction of *it is* uses the apostrophe. Remember:

it's = it is		its = possession
		(and breaks the rules)

Write the correct word in the sentences: **it's   its**

(1) The camel hid _____ treat.

(2) _____ going to be a great play.

The word who's is a contraction that means *who is*. Here is an example:

Who's going to be in the play?

Read the sentence again and see if you could say "Who is" instead of "Who's." In the sentence above, you can replace "Who's" with "Who is" so we know it is a contraction and needs an apostrophe.

The word **whose** is a pronoun. It is a possessive form of *who*. Here is an example:

Whose line is next in the play?

Did you notice that *whose* also breaks the rules? It shows possession but doesn't use an apostrophe. Only the contraction of *who is* uses the apostrophe.

Remember:

who's = who is		whose = possession
		(and breaks the rules)

Write the correct word in the sentences: **who's   whose**

(3) _____ bringing snacks for play practice?

(4) _____ donkey is this?

Figures of Speech: Simile, Metaphor

A figure of speech describes something in a way that is not literal. The meaning is not exactly what is written. It is figurative.

Here is an example:

Ava slept like a baby.

This doesn't mean Ava slept as long as a baby or in the same position a baby would. It means she slept peacefully like a baby sleeps. This is a figure of speech.

A simile is a figure of speech. It compares two different things using the words *like* or *as*.

(**Hint:** The word *simile* is close to the word *similar*. Similar means almost the same.)

Our sentence about Ava sleeping like a baby is a simile. It uses the word *like*.

A simile can also use the word *as*. Here is an example:

This room is as hot as the sun.

This is a figure of speech because the room isn't really as hot as the sun. The simile is used to help the reader understand that it is very hot in the room.

We can make our sentences fun by using similes.

Finish the sentences using a simile. You may use more than one word:

My father is like _____ .

My mother is as _____ .

Write a sentence using the simile **as.**

_____

_____

Write a sentence using the simile **like.**

_____

_____

A metaphor is also a figure of speech. It compares two different things without using the words *like* or *as.*

Here is an example:

My dog is a chicken.

My dog is not a chicken. My dog is a dog. A metaphor is used to mean that my dog is scared of things.

Now it is your turn. Write a sentence using a fun metaphor. Remember, you can't use the words *like* or *as.*

_____

_____

Christmas Star!

The tree is decorated, but the star for the top is missing! See if you can reach the star in the center of the maze.

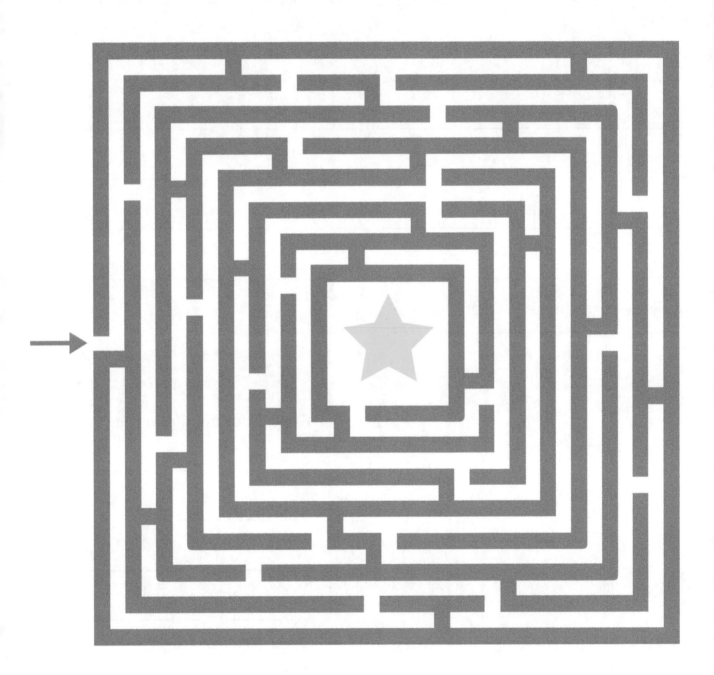

READING COMPREHENSION

Read "Haman's Evil Plot" on pages 112–113 of *101 Favorite Stories from the Bible* with your teacher.

Answer the questions on page 113.

Copy Luke 12:2, then memorize it with your teacher.

_____

_____

_____

_____

Copy the picture on page 113. Color your picture.

Copy the caption from page 113.

_____

_____

_____

_____

_____

_____

_____

-ar, -er, and -or Words

We are going to work with words that end in -ar, -er, and -or.

Learn to spell these words:

> answer, beggar, calendar, chapter, collar, director, doctor,
> labor, motor, polar, proper, sailor, sugar, weather

The spelling words are going on a trip and need to pack. Group the words by how they are spelled and put them in the right suitcases.

(1) -ar words

_____

_____

_____

_____

(2) -er words

_____

_____

_____

_____

(3) -or words

_____

_____

_____

_____

Write a fun sentence using at least two of your -ar spelling words.

_____

_____

Write a fun sentence using at least two of your -er spelling words.

_____

_____

Write a fun sentence using at least two of your -or spelling words.

_____

_____

Be sure to start each sentence with a capital letter and end it with a punctuation mark.

For More Practice:

Write your words in the shape boxes using the worksheet for this lesson available as a free download at masterbooks.com/classroom-aids.

Write your spelling words on notecards. Write one word on each card. You may create right-brain flashcards with your words.

Ask your teacher to read each spelling word. Spell the word out loud and use it in a sentence.

CREATE YOUR OWN DICTIONARY!

Psalm 98

¹O sing to the LORD a new song,
For He has done wonderful things,
His right hand and His holy arm have
   gained the victory for Him.
²The LORD has made known His salvation;
He has revealed His righteousness in the
   sight of the nations.
³He has remembered His lovingkindness
   and His faithfulness to the house of
   Israel;
All the ends of the earth have seen the
   salvation of our God.

⁴Shout joyfully to the LORD, all the earth;
Break forth and sing for joy and sing praises.
⁵Sing praises to the LORD with the lyre,
With the lyre and the sound of melody.
⁶With trumpets and the sound of the horn
Shout joyfully before the King, the LORD.

⁷Let the sea roar and all it contains,
The world and those who dwell in it.
⁸Let the rivers clap their hands,
Let the mountains sing together for joy
⁹Before the LORD, for He is coming to judge
   the earth;
He will judge the world with righteousness
And the peoples with equity.

Comprehension

Were there any words you didn't
understand? Circle them.

TEACHER NOTE

• The teacher should go over with the student the meaning of the circled words in the context of the poem.

NARRATION PRACTICE

(1) What chapter of Psalms did you read?

(2) How many verses are there in this chapter?

(3) Do you remember what a psalm is?

(4) What is this psalm about?

(5) What did you learn about God in this psalm?

(6) What are your favorite verses?

Memorization

Memorize at least three verses of this poem with your teacher. The verses should be in a row and may be picked by you or your teacher.

Write a Psalm

Write a psalm using the first line of the first six verses from Psalm 98. We have given you the first line of each verse. You will write your own line to complete the verse. The first one is done for you as an example.

O sing to the LORD a new song,

The Lord is so good to me!

The LORD has made known His salvation;

_____

He has remembered His lovingkindness and His faithfulness to the house of Israel;

_____

Shout joyfully to the LORD, all the earth;

_____

Sing praises to the LORD with the lyre,

_____

With trumpets and the sound of the horn

_____

INDEPENDENT READING

 **GRAMMAR PRACTICE**

Most – Almost; Sit – Set

We are going to work with the words *almost* and *most*.

| most = the largest amount | almost = nearly |

Study the examples:

Claire was the most thankful student.
Claire almost hugged Mrs. Pruitt.

Fill in the correct word: most   almost

(1) Ava has the _____ lines in the play.

(2) Jin _____ knows all of his lines in the play.

Write a sentence using most.

_____

_____

Write a sentence using almost.

_____

_____

Now we are going to work with the words *sit* and *set*.

sit = rest in an upright position	set = place an object

Study the examples:

Claire had to sit down after hearing the news.
Mrs. Pruitt set the script of the play on the table.

Fill in the correct word: sit   set

(3) Micah loves to _____ behind the sound board.

(4) Claire _____ the manger on the stage.

Write a sentence using sit.

_____

_____

Write a sentence using set.

_____

_____

Writing a Paragraph

Do you remember what a paragraph is? A paragraph is a group of sentences about a specific idea or topic.

Remember, a paragraph should:

- Start on a new line with an indent
- Include at least four sentences
- Start with a topic sentence
- Include 2–3 sentences that give details about the topic
- End with a concluding sentence. This sentence ends the paragraph by saying the topic in another way.

Do you remember our paragraph sandwich? You use a piece of bread for the top and bottom with the good stuff in between.

Write a paragraph about your favorite game, sport, or activity.

Here is an example of a paragraph I wrote about my favorite activity:

I like to go swimming in our pool. I like it best when the water is really warm. It is fun to have races with my boys to see who can swim across the pool the fastest. We also like to get all of the water swirling in one direction until it is like a whirlpool. I have a lot of fun swimming with my family all summer long.

Check off each part as you write your paragraph:

○ Write the topic sentence. Remember to indent your topic sentence.

○ Write 2–3 sentences that give details about your topic. (**Hint:** Tell why the game, sport, or activity is your favorite. Be sure to give important details about it. This might include where the activity or event happened and when, or who was there and why.)

○ Write a concluding sentence.

_____

_____

_____

_____

_____

_____

_____

Did you use a capital letter to start each sentence? Did you use correct punctuation at the end of each sentence? Good job!

 JUST **4** FUN!

Learning about paragraph sandwiches can make you hungry!
Grab a quick snack and have fun completing the following puzzle:

 *fast-food*

H	L	D	O	N	U	T	A	F	R
A	C	P	A	N	C	A	K	E	Q
M	U	N	K	A	R	C	H	S	A
B	P	S	C	B	L	O	E	A	J
U	C	R	O	I	S	S	A	N	T
R	A	D	Y	B	R	E	A	D	N
G	K	P	A	R	I	S	U	W	C
E	E	Q	H	M	U	F	F	I	N
R	F	P	E	L	M	C	S	C	D
I	C	E	C	R	E	A	M	H	Z

READING COMPREHENSION

Read "Isaiah God's Prophet" on pages 114–115 of *101 Favorite Stories from the Bible* with your teacher.

Answer the questions on page 115.

Copy Psalm 123:1, then memorize it with your teacher.

_____

_____

_____

_____

Copy the picture on page 115. Color your picture.

Copy the caption from page 115.

_____

_____

_____

_____

_____

_____

 **SPELLING PRACTICE**

-al, -el, and -le Words

We are going to work with words that end in -al, -el, and -le.

Learn how to spell these words:

> barrel, battle, candle, eagle, final, metal, model,
> nickel, pedal, simple, special, title, total, towel

The spelling words are going on a trip and need to pack. Group the words by how they are spelled and put them in the right suitcases.

(1) -al words

(2) -el words

(3) -le words

Write a fun sentence using at least two of your -al spelling words.

_____

_____

Write a fun sentence using at least two of your -el spelling words.

_____

_____

Write a fun sentence using at least two of your -le spelling words.

_____

_____

Be sure to start each sentence with a capital letter and end it with a punctuation mark.

For More Practice:

Write your words in the shape boxes using the worksheet for this lesson available as a free download at masterbooks.com/classroom-aids.

Write your spelling words on notecards. Write one word on each card. You may create right-brain flashcards with your words.

Ask your teacher to read each spelling word. Spell the word out loud and use it in a sentence.

CREATE YOUR OWN DICTIONARY!

A Brand New Star

The play was about to begin. Claire had her hands full backstage keeping everyone organized, especially the younger kids. She was excited to watch them perform tonight — they had worked so hard! Looking across the room, she noticed Mrs. Pruitt putting the final touches on Ava's costume. Ava looked very nervous! Claire walked over to encourage her. "Ava, your costume is perfect, and you are going to do a great job! You have your lines memorized, so no need to worry. Just go out there and enjoy yourself!" Smiling, Ava said, "Thanks, Claire. I don't think I've ever been so jittery!"

Mrs. Pruitt got everyone's attention, and they joined hands in prayer before she reminded everyone to be as quiet as a mouse unless they were supposed to make noise! With that, she walked out onto the stage to welcome everyone to the performance. Claire made sure everyone was in their proper place. Jin, Ava, and Alexia would be on stage when the curtains opened. She organized the rest of the kids in the order of their appearance and waited for Micah to start the music.

Claire was so busy during the performance that she barely had time to think! She didn't relax until the applause was over, but she knew the play had been a success. She was so thankful to have played a part and had not realized until now how much work went on behind the scenes. Who knew that organizing and encouraging others could be so much fun?

(1)   What was happening backstage before the play began?

(2)   What did Mrs. Pruitt do?

(3)   What did Claire do?

(4)   Why was Claire thankful?

Memorization

Memorize Psalm 107:1 with your teacher.

A *fact* is something that can be proven to be true or false.

An *opinion* is a feeling, belief, or an attitude. It cannot be proven to be true or false.

Study the picture. Write **F** for fact or **O** for opinion next to each sentence about the picture.

(1) _____ The dog is running.

(2) _____ The dog is cute.

(3) _____ The dog is fast.

(4) _____ The dog is wearing a collar.

2nd Quarter Review (Each question is 4 points) Students may use the study sheets in the back of the book.

Draw a line to the correct linking verb for each sentence.

(1) Claire and Ava _____ at church. (present)   are

(2) Claire and Ava _____ at church. (past)   were

(3) Claire _____ excited. (past)   is

(4) Claire _____ excited. (present)   was

(5) I _____ hoping to get a solo in the play. (past)   am

(6) I _____ hoping to get a solo in the play. (present)   was

Fill in the blank with the correct verb: **see   saw   seen**

(7) I have _____ the script of the play.

(8) Mrs. Pruitt _____ Claire.

(9) I _____ Ava and Claire.

Draw a line from each verb to the correct place in time.

(10) **gone**   present

(11) **go**   past

(12) **went**   past with helping verb

Draw a line from the sentence to the correct verb:

(13) I have _____ lunch already.   eat

(14) I _____ my last peach earlier.   eaten

(15) I _____ peaches every day.   ate

Match with the correct word to use:

(16) Singular, far   this
(17) Singular, near   that
(18) Plural, near   these
(19) Plural, far   those

Write the correct word in the sentences: it's   its

(20) The camel hid _____ treat.

(21) _____ going to be a great play.

Write the correct word in the sentences: who's   whose

(22) _____ bringing snacks for play practice?

(23) _____ donkey is this?

Fill in the correct word: most   almost

(24) Ava has the _____ lines in the play.

(25) Jin knows _____ all of his lines in the play.

2nd Quarter Review (Each question is 4 points) Students may use the study sheets in the back of the book.

Match the contractions to the words:

(1) can't   we would

(2) she'll   can not

(3) they're   she will

(4) we'd   they are

Write the name of your state, the abbreviation, and the postal code.

(5) State Name: _____

(6) Abbreviation: _____

(7) Postal Code: _____

Write the abbreviation for each title.

(8) Mister _____   (11) Junior _____

(9) Miss _____   (12) Senior _____

(10) Missus _____

Draw a line from the name of each street to the correct abbreviation:

(13) Boulevard   Tpke.

(14) Highway   Blvd.

(14) Turnpike   Hwy.

Write a synonym and antonym for each word:

(16) **still:** _____ _____

(17) **sting:** _____ _____

Add the suffix -er and -est to the following words:

(18) **nice:** _____ _____

(19) **tall:** _____ _____

(20) **tasty:** _____ _____

(21) **wet:** _____ _____

Match the words to the correct definition:

(22) **figure of speech**   does not use the words like or as

(23) **metaphor**   uses the words like or as

(24) **simile**   describes something in a way that
                              is not literal

(25) Write a paragraph about your favorite animal.

Check off each part as you write your paragraph:

O Write the topic sentence. Remember to indent your topic sentence.

O Write 2–3 sentences that give details about your topic. (**Hint:** Tell why you like your favorite animal. You can also describe it, tell what it eats, or include where it lives.)

O Write a concluding sentence.

_____

_____

_____

_____

_____

_____

_____

Did you use a capital letter to start each sentence? Did you use correct punctuation at the end of each sentence? Good job!

A Musical Mystery!

The Christmas play is about to begin, but there is a problem! The musical instruments are scattered everywhere, and Claire knows what many of them are but isn't sure about some of them. First, choose what the instrument is from the list at the bottom of the page. Then see what number is by the instrument and write the name of the instrument in the crossword puzzle.

o Accordion   o Piano   o Tambourine   o Violin
o Castanets   o Guitar   o Triangle   o Xylophone
o Cello   o Harp   o Trumpet
o Cymbals   o Maracas   o Saxophone
o Drum   o Melodica   o Synthesizer

READING COMPREHENSION

Read "God Speaks Through Jeremiah" on pages 116–117 of *101 Favorite Stories from the Bible* with your teacher.

Answer the questions on page 117.

Copy Ezekiel 6:10, then memorize it with your teacher.

_____

_____

_____

_____

Copy the picture on page 117. Color your picture.

Copy the caption from page 117.

_____

_____

_____

_____

_____

_____

_____

Spelling Review

Use your flashcards to practice your spelling words.

You may:

- Ask someone to quiz you on how to spell the words
- Play spelling games found in the back of the book
- Create your own spelling games
- Use each word in a sentence and say it to your teacher

 **CREATE YOUR OWN DICTIONARY!**

Students may choose their own words this week for their dictionary.

A New Winter Challenge

Micah was surprised when Mr. C. announced this year's memory challenge — all 66 books of the Bible! He was thinking of how difficult that would be when Mr. C. handed out a paper with the books listed in order. He had them separated into five sections and suggested they memorize one section at a time. When Micah saw that it was only about 13 books per week, he began to relax a little.

"As usual, everyone who completes the challenge will receive a prize, but I would like to 'sweeten the deal,' as we used to say, and offer an additional prize if you also memorize the major categories of books in the Bible. These categories are called *genres*. Next year, we will look at these more closely, but for now please know that understanding the genre can help us understand what the Scripture is saying. Anyone who can tell me which books go in each genre will get two prizes." Micah copied them from the board just in case. Law, History, Poetry, Major Prophets, Minor Prophets, Gospel, and Letter. Then he listed which books belonged in each genre.

Micah and Ava were not surprised when Claire said she was excited about the extra challenge — as if it would be fun! Good old Claire. She had the idea for the three of them to work as a team, and they agreed to practice at home each night then recite to each other before class each week. Micah would decide later about the extra memory work.

(1) Why do you think Micah was surprised by Mr. C.'s new memory challenge?

(2) What was the extra challenge?

(3) What was Claire's reaction to the challenge?

Memorization

Mr. C.'s class is going to memorize the books of the Bible. We can too! Work with your teacher over the next two weeks to memorize the following names of books of the Bible.

Genesis	Deuteronomy	1st Samuel	1st Chronicles
Exodus	Joshua	2nd Samuel	2nd Chronicles
Leviticus	Judges	1st Kings	Ezra
Numbers	Ruth	2nd Kings	Nehemiah

TEACHER NOTE
- A list of all the books of the Bible and their genres can be found in the back of the book. It may be helpful to look up a song on the Internet to help memorize the books.

INDEPENDENT READING

Adjectives

Do you remember what an adjective is? An *adjective* describes a noun. Do you remember what a noun is? It is a person, place, or thing. An adjective describes a person, place, or thing.

An adjective can describe:

color, size, shape	tastes, smells, sounds
how many, looks, feels	weather, feelings, behavior

Circle the adjectives in the sentences. Then underline the nouns.

(1) The small white dog ran across the green grass.

(2) The big red ball rolled across the large lawn.

(3) Claire drank the sour lemonade.

(4) The noisy dog barked at the stinky skunk.

(5) The two cute kittens played with the string.

(6) The pokey porcupine hid behind the tree.

(7) The snowy hill made for happy children.

(8) The fast sled carried excited boys.

Write a sentence using at least two adjectives.

_____

_____

Write another sentence using at least two more adjectives.

_____

_____

Do you remember what an article is? An *article* comes before a noun. There are three articles: *a, an, the.* Articles are a type of adjective.

Remember:

Articles come before a noun and are a type of adjective.
Use *a* before words that start with a consonant.
Use *an* before words that start with a vowel.
Use *the* to refer to a specific noun.

Write a sentence using at least two articles:

_____

_____

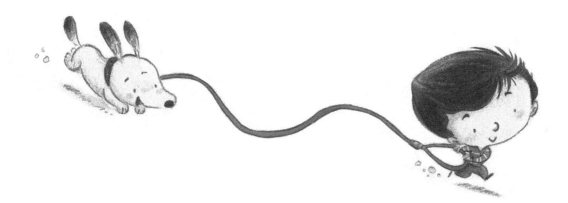

Prefixes

A *prefix* is letters added to the beginning of a word to change the meaning.

Study the meaning of the prefixes:

bi- means two	under- means too little, below
non- means not	mis- means bad or wrong
oct- means eight	over- means too much, above
quad- means four	tri- means three
de- means reduce, remove, get off from, or do the opposite of	

 **TEACHER NOTE** • Prefixes learned in previous levels of *Language Lessons for a Living Education* are in the back of the book. The teacher may want to review the meanings of the prefixes. Students may want to create flashcards to help remember the prefix meanings.

Choose a prefix from the list to create a new word. Write the word. (**Hint:** You may look ahead at your spelling words.) Then tell your teacher the meaning of each word.

(1) angle: _____   (7) sense: _____

(2) crease: _____   (8) cycle: _____

(3) stand: _____   (9) heard: _____

(4) behave: _____

(5) Write a word using the prefix oct-: _____

(6) Write a word using the prefix quad-: _____

READING COMPREHENSION

Read "Three Faithful Boys" on pages 118–119 of *101 Favorite Stories from the Bible* with your teacher.

Answer the questions on page 119.

Copy Matthew 10:28, then memorize it with your teacher.

_____

_____

_____

_____

Copy the picture on page 119. Color your picture.

Copy the caption from page 119.

_____

_____

_____

_____

_____

_____

Prefixes

We are going to work with the prefixes: non-, over-, mis-, de-, under-, bi-, tri-, quad-, and oct-.

Learn to spell these words:

bicycle, decrease, defeat, misbehave, misread, nonsense, octagon, octopus, overdone, overheard, quadrant, triangle, underground, understand

Write the correct spelling word for each meaning.

(1) _____ doesn't make sense; without meaning

(2) _____ heard something without intending to

(3) _____ did not behave; behaved badly

(4) _____ of four parts

(5) _____ over cooked; too much

(6) _____ a vehicle with two wheels

(7) _____ read wrongly

(8) _____ conquer

(9) _____ sea creature with eight legs

(10) _____ to get the meaning of something

(11) _____ to become smaller or fewer

(12) _____ beneath the surface of the ground; in hiding

(13) _____ a shape with eight sides and eight angles

(14) _____ a shape with three sides and three angles

Write a fun sentence using at least two of your spelling words.

_____

_____

Write a fun sentence using at least two more of your spelling words.

_____

_____

Be sure to start each sentence with a capital letter and end it with a punctuation mark.

For More Practice:

Write your words in the shape boxes using the worksheet for this lesson available as a free download at masterbooks.com/classroom-aids.

Write your spelling words on notecards. Write one word on each card. You may create right-brain flashcards with your words.

Ask your teacher to read each spelling word. Spell the word out loud and use it in a sentence.

 CREATE YOUR OWN DICTIONARY!

Title: Return of the Prodigal Son

Scripture Connection

Ask your teacher to read to you Luke 15:11–32 from your Bible.

OBSERVATION SKILLS

(1) Who are the people in this picture?

(2) What is happening in this picture?

(3) How do you think the father feels about his son?

(4) How do you think the son feels about his father?

(5) What colors are used in this picture?

(6) How does this picture make you feel? Why?

(7) What can we learn from this picture and the story it tells?

Rhyming

Write two sentences that rhyme. You may use any rhyming words, but here are some ideas:

should : would : could : wood
send : blend : fend : bend
fruit : suit : toot : mute

_____

_____

INDEPENDENT READING

 **GRAMMAR PRACTICE**

Adverbs

Adverbs are similar to adjectives, but instead of describing a noun, they describe a verb. Adverbs often end in -ly and describe *how, when, where,* or *how often* a verb happens.

Study the example:

> The cat walks quietly.

Do you see the adverb? The adverb is "quietly." It describes the verb "walks." It tells *how* the cat walks. Notice the adverb in this sentence ends with -ly.

An adverb can also tell when, where, or how often a verb happens. Study the examples:

> I ate soup today.
> My cat ran inside.
> I read often.

Do you see the adverb in each of the sentences?

In the first sentence, "today" is an adverb that tells *when* I ate soup.

In the second sentence, "inside" is an adverb that tells *where* my cat ran.

In the third sentence, "often" is the adverb tells *how often* I read.

There are many adverbs. Here is a list of examples to study:

How	When	Where	How Often
gently	early	above	daily
quickly	now	inside	never
quietly	soon	here	often
sadly	tomorrow	outside	usually
safely	yesterday	upstairs	yearly

For each sentence, find the adverb and draw an arrow to the verb it describes:

(1) Claire quickly climbed the tree.

(2) The mail came early.

(3) Jin happily sang a song.

(4) Micah never eats pumpkin pie.

Write a sentence using an adverb that tells **how**.

_____

_____

Write a sentence using an adverb that tells **when**.

_____

_____

Write a sentence using an adverb that tells **where**.

_____

_____

Write a sentence using an adverb that tells **how often**.

_____

_____

Suffixes

A *suffix* is letters added to the end of a word to change the meaning. Study the meaning of the suffixes:

-al means related to, character of
-en means become, made of, resemble, to make
-er means one who, that which
-ial means related to, character of
-ness means condition, state of
-ment means act, process
-or means one who, that which
-tion means act, result, or state of

TEACHER NOTE • Suffixes and rules learned in previous levels of *Language Lessons for a Living Education* are in the back of the book.

Choose a suffix from the list to create a new word. Write the word. Tell your teacher the meaning of each word. (**Hints:** You may need to drop a letter before adding a suffix to words ending in *e* or *y*. Review the Suffix Rules in the back of the book. You may look ahead at your spelling words.)

(1) **farm:** _____   (6) **ill:** _____

(2) **nature:** _____   (7) **wood:** _____

(3) **colony:** _____   (8) **enjoy:** _____

(4) **conduct:** _____

(5) Write a word using the suffix **-tion:** _____

READING COMPREHENSION

Read "Handwriting on the Wall" on pages 120–121 of *101 Favorite Stories from the Bible* with your teacher.

Answer the questions on page 121.

Copy Proverbs 29:23, then memorize it with your teacher.

_____

_____

_____

_____

Copy the picture on page 121. Color your picture.

Copy the caption from page 121.

_____

_____

_____

_____

_____

_____

Books of the Bible

Ava, Claire, and Micah all passed the first Memory Quiz with flying colors! They recited Genesis through Nehemiah in class. Claire's idea for them to work together had been a success. Micah had also learned that Jin's class had the same challenge, so he and Jin practiced together on Saturday. It felt good to be prepared! He told Jin on Saturday that his class also had an extra challenge of memorizing the different genres in the Bible, but he hadn't decided yet if he would do the extra work.

"The different what?" Jin asked.

"Genres," responded Micah. "It's like a category. Mr. C. explained that the Bible is made up of different styles of writing, and we are going to learn what each one is. If we can memorize which books fit into each style, there will be an extra prize."

After they practiced their next books of the Bible, Esther to Joel, the boys began working on their LEGO® version of Solomon's Temple. Mr. C. had helped them come up with a drawing. Then they made a list of the different types and colors of LEGOs® they would need. Both boys had been collecting blocks for the past few weeks and had taken apart some of their previous builds in order to have enough. Today they planned to separate all the LEGOs® by size and color.

"So, you are going to separate the books of the Bible by type, kind of like we are separating these blocks?" Jin asked. "Hey! That's a great way to think about it!" Micah said.

NARRATION PRACTICE

(1) How does the story begin?

(2) How did Micah explain genres to Jin?

(3) What did the boys do after they practiced Esther to Joel?

(4) What thought did Jin have about separating the books of the Bible?

Memorization

Mr. C's class has memorized Genesis to Nehemiah. We can too! Study the list one last time then say them to your teacher.

Genesis	Deuteronomy	1st Samuel	1st Chronicles
Exodus	Joshua	2nd Samuel	2nd Chronicles
Leviticus	Judges	1st Kings	Ezra
Numbers	Ruth	2nd Kings	Nehemiah

Now it is time to work on Esther to Joel, just like Micah and Jin. Practice the books from Esther to Joel. Be sure to remember Genesis to Nehemiah too!

Esther	Ecclesiastes	Lamentations	Joel
Job	Song of Solomon	Ezekiel	
Psalms	Isaiah	Daniel	
Proverbs	Jeremiah	Hosea	

Maps - Subway Stations!

Maps are often used to show us how to get someplace. They can also tell us which bus or route to take to get to where we want to go. Circle the correct answer:

(1) The 27th station is on the:
orange route   green route.

(2) Oakwood Park is on the:
pink route   yellow route.

(3) Jefferson Park is on the:
green route   orange route.

(4) The 96th station is on the:
pink route   purple route.

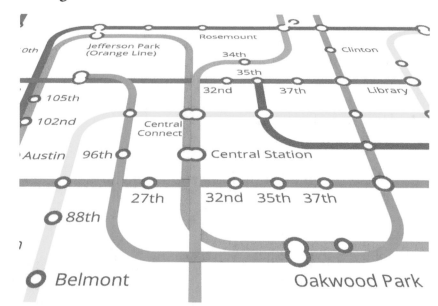

INDEPENDENT READING

SPELLING PRACTICE

Root Words

We are going to work with the root words: *rupt*, *terr*, *geo*, *photo*, *tract*, *meter*, and *metr*.

Learn to spell these words:

> disrupt, erupt, geography, geology, metric, metronome,
> odometer, perimeter, photocopy, photograph,
> subtract, terrain, territory, traction

Write the correct spelling word for each meaning.

(1) _____ explode with fire and noise

(2) _____ based on the meter

(3) _____ a stretch of land

(4) _____ the study of the earth's surface features and people

(5) _____ to break up or cause a disturbance

(6) _____ take away

(7) _____ land belonging to a government or ruler

(8) _____ science dealing with the composition of the earth

(9) _____ a picture made using a camera

(10) _____ grip, pulling of something over a surface such as a road

(11) _____ the boundary of an area or object

(12) _____ a device that marks time

(13) _____ a duplicate copy of something printed or written

(14) _____ an instrument that measures the distance traveled

Write a fun sentence using at least two of your spelling words.

_____

_____

Be sure to start your sentence with a capital letter and end it with a punctuation mark.

For More Practice:

Write your words in the shape boxes using the worksheet for this lesson available as a free download at masterbooks.com/classroom-aids.

Write your spelling words on notecards. Write one word on each card. You may create right-brain flashcards with your words.

Ask your teacher to read each spelling word. Spell the word out loud and use it in a sentence.

CREATE YOUR OWN DICTIONARY!

SPELLING PRACTICE

Homophones
We are going to work with homophones.

Learn to spell these words:

> beat, beet, blew, blue, dear, deer, pain,
> pane, pray, prey, sail, sale, wait, weight

Write the correct words for each set of homophones.

(1)  _____  _____

(2)  _____   _____

(3)  _____   _____

(4)  _____  _____

(5)  _____   _____

(6) _____    _____

(7) _____    _____

Write a fun sentence using at least two of your spelling words.

_____

_____

Write a fun sentence using at least two more of your spelling words.

_____

_____

Be sure to start each sentence with a capital letter and end it with a punctuation mark.

For More Practice:

Write your words in the shape boxes using the worksheet for this lesson available as a free download at masterbooks.com/classroom-aids.

Write your spelling words on notecards. Write one word on each card. You may create right-brain flashcards with your words.

Ask your teacher to read each spelling word. Spell the word out loud and use it in a sentence.

CREATE YOUR OWN DICTIONARY!

The LEGO® Method

Before class the next week, Micah told Ava and Claire what Jin said about the blocks. "I've been thinking; this could help us learn the genres. What do you think about making flashcards out of construction paper? Each book of the Bible would be written on a separate flashcard that is also color coded by their genre, like different colors of LEGO® blocks! We can number them to keep the books in order, but we can also separate them by color when we want to work on the genres."

Claire said, "I love that idea, Micah!" You could see the excitement on Ava's face as she listened. "I was thinking of not doing this part of the challenge, but this makes it sound interesting! We can each make our own set of flashcards to practice with during the week. We could even decorate and trade flashcards with one another to make it fun!" They decided to call their new idea "The LEGO® Method of Memorization," which made them all smile.

As they entered the classroom, Ava realized they had been so busy talking about their new idea they had forgotten to go over today's books of the Bible! Nervously, she began to recite them in her head; *Esther, Job, Psalms, Proverbs, Ecclesiastes, Song of Solomon, Isaiah, Jeremiah, Lamentations, Ezekiel, Daniel, Hosea, and Joel.* Thankfully, she had time to go over them twice and say a quick prayer before Mr. C. came into the room.

NARRATION PRACTICE

(1) What did Micah tell Ava and Claire about?

(2) What did Claire and Ava think of the idea?

(3) What ideas did they have to make it fun?

(4) What did they decide to call their new idea?

(5) Why did Ava say a quick prayer before Mr. C. came into the room?

Memorization

We have memorized Genesis to Nehemiah.

Genesis	Deuteronomy	1st Samuel	1st Chronicles
Exodus	Joshua	2nd Samuel	2nd Chronicles
Leviticus	Judges	1st Kings	Ezra
Numbers	Ruth	2nd Kings	Nehemiah

The class learned the books of Esther to Joel. We can too! Study the list then say the books to your teacher from memory.

Esther	Ecclesiastes	Lamentations	Joel
Job	Song of Solomon	Ezekiel	
Psalms	Isaiah	Daniel	
Proverbs	Jeremiah	Hosea	

Can you say all of the books you have learned so far from Genesis to Joel?

The Sunday school class will now practice the books Amos through Malachi. Work with your teacher over the next couple of weeks to memorize the next set of books.

Amos	Micah	Zephaniah	Malachi
Obadiah	Nahum	Haggai	
Jonah	Habakkuk	Zechariah	

Writing a Story

Using what you have learned in this book, re-write each simple sentence to make it better.

Homonyms

We are going to work with homonyms.

Learn to spell these words:

> fire, bark, foot, rock, iron, change, left,
> pound, bear, trunk, rose, squash, handle, organ

Put the homonyms in alphabetical order. Draw two pictures to show the different meanings of each word. The first one is done for you.

(1) **bark**_____

(5) _____

(2) _____

(6) _____

(3) _____

(7) _____

(4) _____

(8) _____

(9) _____

(12) _____

(10) _____

(13) _____

(11) _____

(14) _____

Pick a spelling word. Write a sentence using the two different meanings of the spelling word.

_____

_____

For More Practice:

Write your words in the shape boxes using the worksheet for this lesson available as a free download at masterbooks.com/classroom-aids.

Write your spelling words on notecards. Write one word on each card. You may create right-brain flashcards with your words.

Ask your teacher to read each spelling word. Spell the word out loud and use it in a sentence.

CREATE YOUR OWN DICTIONARY!

Book Reports

Have you ever read a book that was so good you wanted to tell someone about it? A book report helps us to do just that! We are going to learn about the parts of a story so that we can learn how to write a book report.

A story has a *title*. The title is the name of a book.

A story has an *author*. The author is who wrote the book.

A story has *characters*. Characters are the people or animals in the story.

The *setting* is where and when a story takes place. The setting can be a small place like a kitchen or a big place like a town. A story can take place long ago or just yesterday.

The *plot* is what happens in the story. It tells us what the conflict or the problem is, what happens, and how the conflict or problem is solved. It has a beginning, middle, and end.

The *conclusion*, or ending, answers any questions that need to be answered and wraps up the story.

We can think of a story like a train. It has lots of cars, but it makes up one train.

STORY : title and author CHARACTERS: who SETTING: where and when PLOT: problem with a beginning, middle and end CONCLUSION: ending

Match the parts of a story with what they are:

(1) title   ending

(2) author   problem: beginning, middle, end

(3) characters   where and when

(4) setting   who

(5) plot   the person who wrote it

(6) conclusion   the name of the story

Discuss the parts of a story with your teacher. See if you can find each part of a story in your independent reading book and tell your teacher what they are. Check them off as you find them:

- ○ title
- ○ author
- ○ characters
- ○ setting
- ○ plot
- ○ conclusion

Front and Back!

Now that you have found the different parts of the story in your independent reading book, recreate the cover of the book here. Just draw and color in the details.

Cover Copy!

Look at the back of your independent reading book. Is there a short description on the back telling you about the story in the book? Imagine you are writing a book and want to tell someone enough about it so that they will want to read it. Create your own short description of your book below. Try not to use more than four sentences in your description.

_____

_____

_____

_____

_____

_____

_____

Read "The Angel Gabriel Visits Mary" on pages 130–131 of *101 Favorite Stories from the Bible* with your teacher.

Answer the questions on page 131.

Copy Isaiah 7:14, then memorize it with your teacher.

_____

_____

_____

_____

Copy the picture on page 131. Color your picture.

Copy the caption from page 131.

_____

_____

_____

_____

_____

_____

Flash Cards in the Making!

Claire invited Ava, Micah, and Jin to her house on Saturday to make the flashcards. Even though Jin was not in their class, she thought it might help him with his challenge also. Besides, it was his comment that inspired this whole idea!

She spent the morning getting ready for her friends by gathering craft supplies and taking them to the dining room: markers, scissors, glue, rulers, colored pencils, and the rubber stamp supplies she got for Christmas. The other three would be bringing their favorite stickers and supplies also. Last night, her mom had helped her cut different colors of heavy-duty construction paper into the correct size with a paper trimmer. She put down an old tablecloth and then organized the supplies in the middle of the table.

Claire decided she had better make some snacks. She started by popping some kettle corn and then mixed it into a big bowl with pretzel sticks, banana chips, golden raisins, and M & M candies. Finally, she put some bottles of water in the fridge to chill.

When everyone arrived, they got to work. It was so much fun to share ideas and create their flashcards together. Micah and Jin made their flashcards look like LEGOs® by adding little round stickers in rows on the back side. Claire decorated hers with rubber stamps, and Ava, who loved to draw, made all of hers entirely freehand.

Claire suggested they practice together for tomorrow's class, so they took turns reciting Amos through Malachi until everyone felt like they were ready.

NARRATION PRACTICE

(1) Why did Claire invite Ava, Micah, and Jin to her house?

(2) What did Claire do to get ready?

(3) What did the children do when they arrived?

(4) How does the story end?

Memorization

We have memorized Genesis to Joel.

Genesis	1st Samuel	Esther	Lamentations
Exodus	2nd Samuel	Job	Ezekiel
Leviticus	1st Kings	Psalms	Daniel
Numbers	2nd Kings	Proverbs	Hosea
Deuteronomy	1st Chronicles	Ecclesiastes	Joel
Joshua	2nd Chronicles	Song of Solomon	
Judges	Ezra	Isaiah	
Ruth	Nehemiah	Jeremiah	

The class learned the books of Amos to Malachi. We can too! Study the list then say the books to your teacher from memory.

Amos	Micah	Zephaniah	Malachi
Obadiah	Nahum	Haggai	
Jonah	Habakkuk	Zechariah	

Can you say all the books you have learned so far from Genesis to Malachi? Those are all the books in the Old Testament! Good job!

The Sunday school class will now start on the New Testament. They will practice the books Matthew through Colossians. Work with your teacher over the next couple of weeks to memorize the next set of books.

Matthew	John	1st Corinthians	Ephesians
Mark	Acts	2nd Corinthians	Philippians
Luke	Romans	Galatians	Colossians

Do you remember learning about these parts of speech? If not, it is okay. We will learn about them together.

The eight parts of speech help us create sentences. They help us write fun sentences. They help us tell about things we know.

The eight parts of speech are like tools in your tool box. They help you put your ideas together in a way that people can understand.

Look at the first three parts of speech. Spend some time studying them with your teacher.

PARTS OF SPEECH

○ **noun**

○ **verb**

○ **pronoun**

> **TEACHER NOTE**
>
> • Please discuss the first three parts of speech with your student. This exercise is designed to be a fun way to discover what your student remembers about the parts of speech. It is also designed to help a student understand why they are studying these topics.
> Ask the student: Do you remember what a noun is? Can you give me an example of a noun? Can you use a noun in a sentence? Tell it to me. Continue with this pattern for each concept.
> If a student does not remember a concept, read the concept and use one of the examples in a sentence. You may discuss the concept but do not expect mastery. Simply move on to the next one while encouraging the student. You may want to spend some time this week playing the games in the back of the book that cover the first three parts of speech.
>
> • Create right-brain flashcards with your student for the first three parts of speech.

Book Reports

Do you remember the parts of a story? Our story train can help us remember!

Ask your teacher for the story you started to read in Lesson 24. Today we will work on the Title & Author Engine and the Characters and Setting cars. Fill in the information next to each train about the story.

SETTING:
where and when

_____

_____

_____

_____

_____

_____

_____

_____

TEACHER NOTE

- Students may need some help finding and identifying the title, author, characters, and setting in their story. Assist and encourage the student as needed.

READING COMPREHENSION

Read "Jesus is Born in Bethlehem" on pages 132–133 of *101 Favorite Stories from the Bible* with your teacher.

Answer the questions on page 133.

Copy Isaiah 9:6, then memorize it with your teacher.

_____

_____

_____

_____

Copy the picture on page 133. Color your picture.

Copy the caption from page 133.

_____

_____

_____

_____

_____

_____

Psalm 100

¹Shout joyfully to the LORD, all the earth.

²Serve the LORD with gladness;

Come before Him with joyful singing.

³Know that the LORD Himself is God;

It is He who has made us, and not we ourselves;

We are His people and the sheep of His pasture.

⁴Enter His gates with thanksgiving

And His courts with praise.

Give thanks to Him, bless His name.

⁵For the LORD is good;

His lovingkindness is everlasting

And His faithfulness to all generations.

Comprehension

Were there any words you didn't
understand? Circle them.

 TEACHER NOTE
- The teacher should go over with the student the meaning of the circled words in the context of the psalm.

 NARRATION PRACTICE

(1) What chapter of Psalms did you read?

(2) How many verses are there in this chapter?

(3) What is this psalm about?

(4) What did you learn about God in this psalm?

(5) What are your favorite verses?

Memorization

Memorize at least three verses of this psalm. The verses should be in a row and may be picked by you or your teacher. You may want to try to memorize the whole chapter!

Write a Psalm

Write a psalm that has at least two verses. Each verse should have at least two lines. Remember, a psalm is a song. It praises God. After you write your psalm, think of a tune and sing it!

_____

_____

_____

_____

_____

INDEPENDENT READING

TEACHER NOTE
• The student may continue to read the story used for the lesson on book reports or a new story may be chosen. Keep the story used for the book report lesson on hand for future lessons.

Eight Parts of Speech

Let's look at the eight parts of speech again. Do you still remember the first three parts of speech you studied last time? They are the noun, pronoun, and verb. Today we are going to study two more parts of speech — the adjective and adverb. We will also study the last three parts of speech — prepositions, conjunctions, and interjections. Let's get started! Be sure to study the chart again.

Noun   person, place, thing

Examples: cat, yard, ball

Verb   shows action or state of being.
Examples: ran, jump, is, am

Pronoun   takes the place of a noun.
Examples: he, she, it

Adjective   describes a noun or pronoun. It tells what kind, how many, which one.
Examples: red, five, bumpy

Adverb   describes a verb, adjective, or another adverb. It tells when, where, how, or how often.
Examples: after, inside, gently, always

Preposition   describes a relationship between a noun or pronoun and another word that follows it.
Examples: to, for, with

Interjection   expresses strong feeling or emotion. Often followed by an exclamation point.
Examples: Hi! Ouch! Yes!

Conjunction   joins words or phrases.
Examples: and, or, but

We already learned about some of the tools we can use to create great sentences. We learned about nouns, pronouns, and verbs. Now let's see what we know about adjectives, adverbs, prepositions, conjunctions, and interjections. Spend some time studying them with your teacher.

 **TEACHER NOTE**

- Please discuss adjectives, adverbs, prepositions, conjunctions, and interjections with your student. This will allow students to think through the concepts and express what they know.
  Ask the student: Do you remember what an adjective is? Can you give me an example of an adjective? Can you use an adjective in a sentence? Tell it to me. Continue this pattern to discuss adverbs, prepositions, conjunctions, and interjections.
  If a student does not remember a concept, read the concept and use one of the examples in a sentence. You may discuss the concept, but do not expect mastery. Simply move on to the next one while encouraging the student. You may want to spend some time this week playing the games in the back of the book that cover adjectives, adverbs, prepositions, conjunctions, and interjections.

- Create right-brain flashcards with your student for adjectives, adverbs, prepositions, conjunctions, and interjections.

Book Reports

Do you remember the parts of a story? Our story train can help us remember!

Ask your teacher for the story you started to read in Lesson 24. Today we will work on the Plot car and the Conclusion Caboose. Fill in the information next to each train about the story.

PLOT: *problem the beginning*

_____

_____

PLOT: *problem the middle*

_____

_____

PLOT: *problem the end*

_____

_____

_____

CONCLUSION: *ending*

_____

_____

TEACHER NOTE
• Students may need some help finding and identifying the plot and conclusion in their story. Assist and encourage the student as needed.

READING COMPREHENSION

Read "The Shepherds and the Wise Men" on pages 134–135 of *101 Favorite Stories from the Bible* with your teacher.

Answer the questions on page 135.

Copy John 3:16, then memorize it with your teacher.

_____

_____

_____

_____

Copy the picture on page 135. Color your picture.

Copy the caption from page 135.

_____

_____

_____

_____

_____

_____

Three Syllable Words

We are going to work with words that have three syllables.

Helpful hints:

Divide the word into syllables, noting unstressed syllables. Watch for spelling patterns.

Learn to spell these words:

> compromise, direction, suddenly, following, afternoon,
> holiday, family, behavior, alphabet, internet,
> navigate, document, remember, edible

Write the spelling words in alphabetical order.

(1) _____

(2) _____

(3) _____

(4) _____

(5) _____

(6) _____

(7) _____

(8) _____

(9) _____

(10) _____

(11) _____

(12) _____

(13) _____

(14) _____

Write a fun sentence using at least two of your spelling words.

_____

_____

Write another fun sentence using two more of your spelling words.

_____

_____

Be sure to start each sentence with a capital letter and end it with a punctuation mark.

For More Practice:

Write your words in the shape boxes using the worksheet for this lesson available as a free download at masterbooks.com/classroom-aids.

Write your spelling words on notecards. Write one word on each card. You may create right-brain flashcards with your words.

Ask your teacher to read each spelling word. Spell the word out loud and use it in a sentence.

 **CREATE YOUR OWN DICTIONARY!**

A Special Cornerstone

Micah and Jin were spending their Saturday working on Solomon's Temple. Jin's parents had invited Mr. Cunningham to lunch after church the next day, and they wanted to show him their progress.

They set up portable building trays on a table and discussed where to place the first block. Micah wanted to start in the middle and build outward, but Jin wanted to start at the corner of the building. He said all ancient buildings started with a special cornerstone. This foundation stone was used as a guide for all the other stones that would be placed. It would help keep the building straight and solid.

Micah didn't think they *needed* a cornerstone since the LEGO® tray and blocks would keep their building straight and solid, but he did think it was a cool idea to try and build in the same manner the original builders of the temple used. They began by measuring to determine the best place to lay the foundation block so the building would end up in the center of the trays. They referred to the plan Mr. C. had helped them draw to get the right measurements for the building, and then they needed to measure the available space on the trays. *I guess math does come in handy,* thought Micah.

The boys realized that a lot of thought and skill goes into designing a building from scratch. Once they found their starting point, they began to build. As they worked, they practiced the books of the Bible they would need to recite in tomorrow's class.

NARRATION PRACTICE

(1) How did Micah and Jin spend their Saturday?

(2) What is a cornerstone and why did Jin think they needed one?

(3) What did Micah think about using a cornerstone?

(4) What did the boys learn about designing a building?

Memorization

We have memorized Genesis to Malachi.

Genesis	1st Kings	Ecclesiastes	Obadiah
Exodus	2nd Kings	Song of Solomon	Jonah
Leviticus	1st Chronicles	Isaiah	Micah
Numbers	2nd Chronicles	Jeremiah	Nahum
Deuteronomy	Ezra	Lamentations	Habakkuk
Joshua	Nehemiah	Ezekiel	Zephaniah
Judges	Esther	Daniel	Haggai
Ruth	Job	Hosea	Zechariah
1st Samuel	Psalms	Joel	Malachi
2nd Samuel	Proverbs	Amos	

The class learned Matthew to Colossians. Study the list; recite the books from memory. Can you say all of the books you have learned so far from Genesis to Colossians?

Matthew	John	1st Corinthians	Ephesians
Mark	Acts	2nd Corinthians	Philippians
Luke	Romans	Galatians	Colossians

The Sunday school class will now practice the books Amos through Malachi. Work with your teacher over the next week to memorize the last set of books.

1st Thessalonians	Titus	1st Peter	3rd John
2nd Thessalonians	Philemon	2nd Peter	Jude
1st Timothy	Hebrews	1st John	Revelation
2nd Timothy	James	2nd John	

TEACHER NOTE
• There is only one week between stories. You may want to allow two weeks to memorize the books and only one week to memorize the genres.

INDEPENDENT READING

3rd Quarter Review (Each question is 4 points) Students may use the study sheets in the back of the book.

(1)   Write a sentence using at least two adjectives. (**Hint:** An adjective describes a noun.)

_____

_____

Match the articles to the correct answer.

(2) a   used before words that start with a vowel

(3) an   used to refer to a specific noun

(4) the   used before words that start with a consonant

(5)   Write a sentence using an adverb. (**Hint:** An adverb tells how, when, where, or how often.)

_____

_____

In the sentences below, underline the prepositional phrase and then circle the preposition. Finally, write **OP** above the object of the preposition.

(6) The squirrel ran into the tree.

(7) The boys went inside the house.

(8)   Write a sentence using a prepositional phrase. (**Hint:** You may use a preposition of location or time.)

_____

_____

Match the homophones, homonyms, and homographs to each correct description. (**Hint:** Each word has more than one answer and one answer will not be used.)

sound the same

sound different

(9) homophones

(10) homonyms

(11) homographs

same meaning

different meaning

same spelling

different spelling

Match the homophones to the correct meaning:

(12) to

(13) too

(14) two

also or a lot

a number

direction

(15) there

(16) their

(17) they're

a contraction-they are

a place

belonging to others

Match the eight Parts of Speech to the correct definition:

(18) noun

(19) pronoun

(20) verb

(21) adjective

(22) adverb

(23) preposition

(24) conjunction

(25) interjection

shows action or state of being

takes the place of a noun

person, place, or thing

describes a verb, adjective, or another adverb. It tells when, where, how, or how often.

describes a noun or pronoun. It tells what kind, how many, or which one.

expresses strong feeling or emotion and is often followed by an exclamation point

joins words or phrases

describes a relationship between a noun or pronoun and another word that follows it

3rd Quarter Review (Each question is 5 points) Students may use the study sheets in the back of the book.

Match the prefix with the correct definition. (**Hint:** You will use one definition twice.)

(1)	bi-	bad or wrong
(2)	non-	too much, above
(3)	oct-	three
(4)	quad-	not
(5)	under-	eight
(6)	de-	four
(7)	mis-	too little, below
(8)	over-	two
(9)	tri-	reduce, remove, get off from, or do the opposite of

Match the suffix with the correct definition. (**Hint:** You will use two definitions twice.)

(10)	-al	
(11)	-en	act, result, or state of
(12)	-er	act, process
(13)	-ial	related to, character of
(14)	-ness	become, made of, resemble, to make
(15)	-ment	one who, that which
(16)	-or	condition, state of
(17)	-tion	

Match the root word with the correct definition.

(18) rupt   earth, ground, or soil

(19) terr   break or burst

(20) geo   measure

(21) photo   land

(22) tract   light

(23) meter or metr   pull or drag

(24) What is the setting of a story? _____

_____

(25) What is the plot of a story? _____

_____

_____

_____

_____

Bonus: (10 points)

Write a paragraph describing your room. Be sure to tell what is in your room. You may want to tell what you like about your room.

Check off each part as you write your paragraph:

    O Write the topic sentence. Remember to indent your topic sentence. (2 points)

    O Write 2–3 sentences that give details about your topic. (6 points)

    O Write a concluding sentence. (2 points)

_____

_____

_____

_____

_____

_____

_____

_____

_____

_____

Did you use a capital letter to start each sentence? Did you use correct punctuation at the end of each sentence? Good job!

READING COMPREHENSION

Read "The Boy Jesus at the Temple" on pages 136–137 of *101 Favorite Stories from the Bible* with your teacher.

Answer the questions on page 137.

Copy Colossians 2:3, then memorize it with your teacher.

_____

_____

_____

_____

Copy the picture on page 137. Color your picture.

Copy the caption from page 137.

_____

_____

_____

_____

_____

_____

Spelling Review

Use your flashcards to practice your spelling words.

You may:

- Ask someone to quiz you on how to spell the words
- Play spelling games found in the back of the book
- Create your own spelling games
- Use each word in a sentence and say it to your teacher

CREATE YOUR OWN DICTIONARY!

Students may choose their own words this week for their dictionary.

Lunch at Jin's House

Micah was hungry as his family made their way to Jin's house for lunch. He was excited to show Mr. C. their project, but first things first. Jin's mom was making lasagna because Mr. C. had lived in Italy for a few years. Micah LOVED Italian food!

As everyone talked over lunch, the boys realized that Mr. C. had lived in lots of different countries and had eaten many things that did not sound appetizing to Micah at all. He was thankful Jin's mom had chosen an Italian theme for today's lunch! He began to wonder, *What kind of food does Carlos eat? Do they like pizza and spaghetti in Honduras?* He would have to write Carlos soon and ask him.

After lunch, they all went to see the temple. The boys explained their process and how they had started with the cornerstone. Mr. C. explained just how important the cornerstone was in that type of construction. Then he told them about a much deeper meaning for this stone. "Today, the people of God are considered the temple and Jesus Christ is our Foundation and Cornerstone. He is what holds us together, keeps us strong, and helps us stay in line with His Word. If we build our lives on this foundation, we will stand strong — just like a well-built building."

"I didn't know we could learn so much about God from LEGOs®!" Jin said. His dad responded, "Actually, we can learn about God by studying anything. Even math." Micah and Jin looked at each other with a smile — *yep, even math.*

(1) Why was Jin's mom making lasagna?

(2) What did the boys learn about Mr. C.?

(3) What did Mr. C. explain about the cornerstone?

(4) What did Jin's dad say they can learn about God from?

Memorization

We have memorized Genesis to Colossians.

Genesis	2nd Chronicles	Daniel	Matthew
Exodus	Ezra	Hosea	Mark
Leviticus	Nehemiah	Joel	Luke
Numbers	Esther	Amos	John
Deuteronomy	Job	Obadiah	Acts
Joshua	Psalms	Jonah	Romans
Judges	Proverbs	Micah	1st Corinthians
Ruth	Ecclesiastes	Nahum	2nd Corinthians
1st Samuel	Song of Solomon	Habakkuk	Galatians
2nd Samuel	Isaiah	Zephaniah	Ephesians
1st Kings	Jeremiah	Haggai	Philippians
2nd Kings	Lamentations	Zechariah	Colossians
1st Chronicles	Ezekiel	Malachi	

The class learned the books of 1st Thessalonians to Revelation. We can too! Study the list then say the books to your teacher from memory.

1st Thessalonians	Titus	1st Peter	3rd John
2nd Thessalonians	Philemon	2nd Peter	Jude
1st Timothy	Hebrews	1st John	Revelation
2nd Timothy	James	2nd John	

Can you say all of the books you have learned so far from Genesis to Revelation? That is all the books of the Bible! Great job!

TEACHER NOTE
• Now that the student knows the books of the Bible, you may want to do sword drills. See instructions in the games section in the back of the book.

The Sunday school class will now learn the genres. Work with your teacher over the next couple of weeks to memorize the genres.

Law	Poetry	Minor Prophets	Letter
Genesis	Job	Hosea	Romans
Exodus	Psalms	Joel	1st Corinthians
Leviticus	Proverbs	Amos	2nd Corinthians
Numbers	Ecclesiastes	Obadiah	Galatians
Deuteronomy	Song of Solomon	Jonah	Ephesians
		Micah	Philippians
History	**Major Prophets**	Nahum	Colossians
Joshua	Isaiah	Habakkuk	1st Thessalonians
Judges	Jeremiah	Zephaniah	2nd Thessalonians
Ruth	Lamentations	Haggai	1st Timothy
1st Samuel	Ezekiel	Zechariah	2nd Timothy
2nd Samuel	Daniel	Malachi	Titus
1st Kings			Philemon
2nd Kings		**Gospel**	Hebrews
1st Chronicles		Matthew	James
2nd Chronicles		Mark	1st Peter
Ezra		Luke	2nd Peter
Nehemiah		John	1st John
Esther			2nd John
		History	3rd John
		Acts	Jude
			Revelation

TEACHER NOTE
• There are many ways to classify the genres of Scripture. We have used the classification found on the Answers in Genesis website.

INDEPENDENT READING

Genres are based on *Books of the Bible Flashcards* from Answers in Genesis.

Review: Nouns, Pronouns

A noun is a person, place, or thing. A proper noun names a person, place, or thing. Proper names include the days of the week, months, and holidays. A proper noun begins with a capital letter.

Write a proper noun for each common noun.

state: _____   month: _____

boy: _____   myself: _____

A possessive noun shows ownership. We add 's to the end of a noun to show that it is a possessive noun.

When a possessive noun is plural and ends with s, we simply add an apostrophe after the s.

Remember: *Singular* means one. *Plural* means more than one.

Write the plural possessive noun for each noun:

(1) **tree:** _____   (2) **dog:** _____

Do you remember what a pronoun is? A *pronoun* takes the place of a noun. When a pronoun takes the place of more than one noun, it is called a *plural pronoun*.

Study the chart:

Singular Pronouns	Plural Pronouns
I, you, it	us
she, her	we
he, him	them

Write a sentence using a singular pronoun.

_____

_____

Write a sentence using a plural pronoun.

_____

_____

Do you remember what an antecedent is?

The antecedent is the noun or nouns the pronoun stands for.

Study the examples:

Micah and Jin are studying together.
They are studying together.

(3) What are the antecedents the pronoun *They* stands for? _____

Do you remember what *possessive* means? It means ownership.

We do not add an apostrophe or apostrophe *s* to *possessive pronouns*.

Study the chart:

Possessive Pronouns
my, your, his, her, its, our, their

Write a sentence using a possessive pronoun.

_____

_____

What possessive pronoun did you use in your sentence? _____

What belongs to the possessive pronoun you used? _____

Study the chart:

> ## Pronouns that can Stand Alone
> ## mine, yours, ours, his, hers, theirs

Note: The pronoun *his* can be used with a regular possessive pronoun, and it can stand alone.

We are going to use the pronoun *his* in two ways. Study the examples:

Jin showed us his flashcards.

In this sentence, the pronoun *his* is used to show ownership of the flashcards.

They are his.

Write a sentence using a pronoun that can stand alone.

_____

_____

 **Count the Words!**

(4) See how many times you can find the word "bird" in this puzzle! Note the example. The word may not always be in a straight line, but it has to follow the letter order in the word B-I-R-D.

B	Q	J	I	J	S	W	B
D	B	T	W	B	I	R	D
O	I	E	A	U	D	J	I
J	R	D	I	R	D	Y	D
I	N	F	B	K	B	T	R
U	M	D	J	O	I	D	I
B	I	R	Y	H	R	L	B
G	Q	V	J	B	D	E	I

Review: Sentences, Punctuation

Start the first word of each sentence with a capital letter and end it with a punctuation mark.

There are four types of sentences:

Imperative:	gives a command; ends with a period
Declarative:	makes a statement; ends with a period
Exclamatory:	expresses strong emotion; ends with an exclamation point
Interrogative:	asks a question; ends with a question mark

Correctly match the four types of sentences:

(1) Imperative   asks a question

(2) Declarative   expresses strong emotion

(3) Exclamatory   makes a statement

(4) Interrogative   gives a command

Write the correct punctuation after each sentence type.

(5) Imperative _____

(6) Declarative _____

(7) Exclamatory _____

(8) Interrogative _____

Do you remember what an interjection is? They are words added to a sentence that express emotion. Here are some examples:

Yay!   Ouch!   Wow!   Hurray!   Yes!   Stop!

Write a sentence using an interjection.

_____

_____

Do you remember how to use commas? We use a comma when we write a list of things in a sentence. We also use a comma when we address someone. A comma comes after each item in a list.

Put commas in the right place in each sentence. (**Hint:** Some sentences have more than one comma.)

(9) Did Claire make the flashcards Micah?

(10) Micah washed the dishes folded his clothes and made his bed.

(11) Ava did you eat popcorn?

(12) How long Jin did it take to memorize the books of the Bible?

What's for Lunch?

There are a lot of different places you can go to get lunch and a lot of different kinds of food that you like. Let's see if you can find your way to the "I'm Here Buddy" burger and fries. Use a marker to show your path on the maze map.

READING COMPREHENSION

Read "Jesus Is Baptized and Tempted" on pages 138–139 of *101 Favorite Stories from the Bible* with your teacher.

Answer the questions on page 139.

Copy Hebrews 4:15, then memorize it with your teacher.

_____

_____

_____

_____

Copy the picture on page 139. Color your picture.

Copy the caption from page 139.

_____

_____

_____

_____

_____

_____

 **SPELLING PRACTICE**

Blends

We are going to work with words that have the blends *ng*, *nk*, *nt*, *pt*, *sk*, and *st*.

Learn to spell these words:

> belong, bling, blanket, drink, frequent, saint, tempt,
> swept, scared, scope, skirt, skunk, starve, least

Write the spelling words in alphabetical order.

(1) _____

(2) _____

(3) _____

(4) _____

(5) _____

(6) _____

(7) _____

(8) _____

(9) _____

(10) _____

(11) _____

(12) _____

(13) _____

(14) _____

Write silly sentences until you have used all the spelling words. Put as many spelling words as you can into each sentence.

_____

_____

_____

_____

_____

_____

Circle each of the spelling words in your sentences.

For More Practice:

Write your words in the shape boxes using the worksheet for this lesson available as a free download at masterbooks.com/classroom-aids.

Write your spelling words on notecards. Write one word on each card. You may create right-brain flashcards with your words.

Ask your teacher to read each spelling word. Spell the word out loud and use it in a sentence.

 CREATE YOUR OWN DICTIONARY!

Title: The Good Samaritan

Artist: Christen Dalsgaard

Scripture Connection

Ask your teacher to read to you Luke 10:25–37 from your Bible.

 **OBSERVATION SKILLS**

(1) Who are the people shown in the front of this picture?

(2) Who are the people in the background of this picture?

(3) What is happening in this picture?

(4) What colors are used in this picture?

(5) How does this picture make you feel? Why?

(6) What can we learn from this picture and the story it tells?

Comprehension

A parable is a story that Jesus told to teach us a lesson.

Write four sentences about the parable of the Good Samaritan. (**Hint:** Think through the story and answer the questions, either to yourself or out loud to your teacher, before you write them down.)

What happened first?

_____

_____

What happened next?

_____

_____

What happened after that?

_____

_____

What happened last?

_____

_____

 **Plural Nouns**

Remember:

> Plural means more than one.

We make many words plural by adding *s*.

When a word ends in a vowel and *y*, we add *s*.

When a word ends in a vowel and *o*, we add *s*.

Remember:

plural = add s	ends in s, ss, sh, ch, z, or x = add es

vowel + y, add s key = keys	vowel + o, add s radio = radios	consonant + o, add es hero = heroes

There are two exceptions to this rule!

piano = pianos	photo = photos

Add -s or -es to the end of the words to make them plural. Study the rules if you aren't sure.

(1) waltz_____

(2) rock_____

(3) box_____

(4) hero_____

(5) bush_____

(6) photo_____

(7) chimney_____

(8) church_____

(9) radio_____

(10) fuss_____

When a word ends in the letter *f* or *fe*, we make it plural by changing the *f* or *fe* to *v* and then adding *es*.

There are two exceptions to this rule!

roof = roofs	cliff = cliffs

When a word ends in a consonant and the letter *y*, we make it plural by changing the *y* to *i* and then adding *es*.

Change these words to make them plural.

(11) **calf** _____   (12) **mystery** _____

Some plural nouns don't follow the rules! Do you remember what those nouns are called? They are **irregular nouns.**

Match the singular nouns with the correct plural noun.

Singular	Plural		Singular	Plural
(13) **woman**	people		(21) **deer**	corn
(14) **child**	women		(22) **fish**	seaweed
(15) **person**	children		(23) **sheep**	moose
(16) **goose**	oxen		(24) **moose**	sheep
(17) **mouse**	cacti		(25) **corn**	deer
(18) **ox**	octopi		(26) **seaweed**	fish
(19) **octopus**	geese			
(20) **cactus**	mice			

Review: Sentences — Subject, Predicate, Conjunctions, Combining

A sentence must express a complete thought. It must have a subject and a predicate. Remember:

> Subject tells who or what the sentence is about.

> Predicate tells what the subject does or is.

Circle the sentences that are correctly written.

(1) Micah was nervous about his new class?

(2) Dad said Micah would learn a life lesson.

(3) Alexia wanted

(4) micah might make some new friends.

(5) He had a lot on his mind!

Underline the subject and circle the predicate of each sentence.

(6) Micah wanted Jin in his class.

(7) Micah was the youngest in his class.

Combining sentences is fun, and it helps us share our ideas in a better way.

(8) Combine the two sentences into one. (**Hint:** You will need to use a plural pronoun.)

Micah went to his class.
Claire went to her class.

_____

_____

Do you remember what a conjunction is? Conjunctions are words that join two words or phrases together. Here are some common conjunctions:

for   and   nor   but   or   yet   so

We can memorize this list of common conjunctions by looking at the first letter of each word:

for   and   nor   but   or   yet   so

(9) Write the first letter of each word here:

_____ _____ _____ _____ _____ _____ _____

That is a silly word that can help us remember some conjunctions. We call this an *acronym*. An acronym is letters that stand for words. We can use acronyms to help us remember things.

Use the conjunctions above to complete the sentences.

(10) You can either go swimming _____ weed the garden.

(11) I like spring, _____ I love fall.

(12) It is snowing heavily, _____ I can go sledding.

(13) Combine the two sentences using a conjunction.

I like apples.
I love peaches.

_____

_____

Wacky Word Find Time!

See if you can find the names of all the rooms in the house and places around it. This is a zig zag word search puzzle. Words go left, right, up, down, not diagonally, and can bend at a right angle. There are no unused letters in the word search grid and every letter is only used once.

House

```
A  D  I  N  I  N  G  R  R  A
T  R  A  L  L  E  C  O  A  G
T  I  C  N  K  I  P  O  G  E
L  A  U  U  Y  T  O  M  L  I
M  Y  N  R  R  C  R  C  H  V
O  A  D  S  E  H  E  N  H  I
O  R  R  A  S  E  N  G  A  N
R  D  Y  B  B  M  E  A  L  G
H  T  A  B  E  E  D  R  L  R
M  O  O  R  D  N  T  M  O  O
```

- o Attic
- o Basement
- o Bathroom
- o Bedroom
- o Cellar
- o Dining Room
- o Garage
- o Garden
- o Hall
- o Kitchen
- o Laundry
- o Living Room
- o Nursery
- o Porch
- o Yard

READING COMPREHENSION

Read "Jesus Begins His Ministry" on pages 140–141 of *101 Favorite Stories from the Bible* with your teacher.

Answer the questions on page 141.

Copy John 1:14, then memorize it with your teacher.

_____

_____

_____

_____

Copy the picture on page 141. Color your picture.

Copy the caption from page 141.

_____

_____

_____

_____

_____

_____

Blends

We are going to work with words with the blends *sh*, *th*, *ch*, and *tch*.

Learn to spell these words:

> attach, brush, challenge, change, chicken, kitchen, latch,
> preach, shape, sharpen, stretch, thank, thirsty, watch

Create your own word search with your spelling words.

- o attach
- o brush
- o challenge
- o change
- o chicken
- o kitchen
- o latch
- o preach
- o shape
- o sharpen
- o stretch
- o thank
- o thirsty
- o watch

Write a fun sentence using at least two of your spelling words.

_____

_____

Write another fun sentence using two more of your spelling words.

_____

_____

Be sure to start each sentence with a capital letter and end it with a punctuation mark.

For More Practice:

Write your words in the shape boxes using the worksheet for this lesson available as a free download at masterbooks.com/classroom-aids.

Write your spelling words on notecards. Write one word on each card. You may create right-brain flashcards with your words.

Ask your teacher to read each spelling word. Spell the word out loud and use it in a sentence.

CREATE YOUR OWN DICTIONARY!

A Strong Foundation

Claire said a silent prayer for Micah as he recited the genres in class. She and Ava had already finished. Both of them had done well, even though this year's memory work had been challenging. *I guess that's why they call it a **challenge**,* she thought.

She breathed a sigh of relief when Micah finished and thought to herself how much more confident he had been this year. It felt really good to see her friend succeed. She recognized how much they had both grown. Not getting a major part in the Christmas play had been hard, but the Lord helped her find joy in seeing others step out in faith. Ava had learned that God was always with her, even when she was center stage! Claire smiled as she remembered Ava beaming when the play was over.

When Micah told her what Mr. C. said about the importance of a strong foundation, she realized she had learned a similar lesson herself. The audience never saw all the work that went on behind the scenes, but without it, the play would not have happened. The script, music, costume designers, set crew, sound, and lighting team all came together as the foundation to a great performance.

Then she remembered her parents saying that Christ was the foundation of their family. *Wow, I never understood the importance of a strong foundation before,* she thought as an old Sunday school song came to mind, "The wise man built his house upon the Rock." *Lord, help me to be wise.*

NARRATION PRACTICE

(1) Why did Claire say a prayer for Micah?

(2) How had Micah, Claire, and Ava grown?

(3) What did Claire learn about having a strong foundation?

(4) What song came to Claire's mind and what did she pray?

Memorization

We have memorized Genesis to Revelation. That is all the books of the Bible! Can you say them to your teacher?

Genesis	Job	Habakkuk	1st Thessalonians
Exodus	Psalms	Zephaniah	2nd Thessalonians
Leviticus	Proverbs	Haggai	1st Timothy
Numbers	Ecclesiastes	Zechariah	2nd Timothy
Deuteronomy	Song of Solomon	Malachi	Titus
Joshua	Isaiah	Matthew	Philemon
Judges	Jeremiah	Mark	Hebrews
Ruth	Lamentations	Luke	James
1st Samuel	Ezekiel	John	1st Peter
2nd Samuel	Daniel	Acts	2nd Peter
1st Kings	Hosea	Romans	1st John
2nd Kings	Joel	1st Corinthians	2nd John
1st Chronicles	Amos	2nd Corinthians	3rd John
2nd Chronicles	Obadiah	Galatians	Jude
Ezra	Jonah	Ephesians	Revelation
Nehemiah	Micah	Philippians	
Esther	Nahum	Colossians	

TEACHER NOTE

- Now that the student knows the books of the Bible, you may want to do sword drills. See instructions in the games section in the back of the book.

The Sunday school class learned the genres. We can too! Study the list, then say the genres to your teacher.

Law	Poetry	Minor Prophets	Letter
Genesis	Job	Hosea	Romans
Exodus	Psalms	Joel	1st Corinthians
Leviticus	Proverbs	Amos	2nd Corinthians
Numbers	Ecclesiastes	Obadiah	Galatians
Deuteronomy	Song of Solomon	Jonah	Ephesians
		Micah	Philippians
History	**Major Prophets**	Nahum	Colossians
Joshua	Isaiah	Habakkuk	1st Thessalonians
Judges	Jeremiah	Zephaniah	2nd Thessalonians
Ruth	Lamentations	Haggai	1st Timothy
1st Samuel	Ezekiel	Zechariah	2nd Timothy
2nd Samuel	Daniel	Malachi	Titus
1st Kings			Philemon
2nd Kings		**Gospel**	Hebrews
1st Chronicles		Matthew	James
2nd Chronicles		Mark	1st Peter
Ezra		Luke	2nd Peter
Nehemiah		John	1st John
Esther			2nd John
		History	3rd John
		Acts	Jude
			Revelation

INDEPENDENT READING

Genres are based on Books of the Bible Flashcards from Answers in Genesis.

Review: Prepositions

Do you remember what a preposition is? A preposition is a word that links a noun (or pronoun) to another word in the sentence. It shows a relationship between a noun and another word.

There are many prepositions. Some prepositions show location:

above	on	inside	in
below	off	outside	to
over	before	with	into
under	after	through	by
behind	beside	between	near

Some prepositions can refer to time:

at	of	until	from
on	to	after	upon
in	since	before	past
by	during	through	about

Write a sentence using a prepositional phrase of location.

_____

_____

_____

Write a sentence using a prepositional phrase of time.

_____

_____

The noun (or pronoun) the preposition refers to is called the *object of the preposition*.

In the sentences below, underline the prepositional phrase then circle the preposition. Finally, write **OP** above the object of the preposition.

(1) Micah went into his room.

(2) Claire studied during lunch.

Prepositions of Location

Write the preposition of location that describes the relationship of the cat and the ball.

before above in between under near on beside behind

(3) _____

(6) _____

(9) _____

(4) _____

(7) _____

(10) _____

(5) _____

(8) _____

(11) _____

Fill in the blanks with the correct prepositions from the box.

on	in	near	behind	over

(12) The dog is _____ the dog house.

(13) The bird is _____ the roof.

(14) The butterflies are flying _____ the pond.

(15) The duck is swimming _____ the pond.

(16) The fish live _____ the pond.

(17) The frog is hiding _____ the stone.

(18) The duck is _____ the fish.

Review: Quotation Marks

Quotation marks are used to show exactly what someone said.

When we use a quote in a sentence, there are a few things we need to make sure we do.

Use quotation marks before and after the quote.

Use a comma after the last word before the quotation.

Use a capital letter to start the quotation.

If a quote comes before the person who spoke, use a comma after the quote and before the ending quotation marks.

Add quotation marks to the sentences below. (**Hint:** They go before and after a direct quote.)

(1) I better get back to my class said Jin as he slowly left the room.

(2) Claire asked Micah, did you show Jin the Temple?

Write a sentence using a quotation.

_____

_____

READING COMPREHENSION

Read "Jesus and the Samaritan Woman" on pages 142–143 of *101 Favorite Stories from the Bible* with your teacher.

Answer the questions on page 143.

Copy John 7:38, then memorize it with your teacher.

_____

_____

_____

_____

Copy the picture on page 143. Color your picture.

Copy the caption from page 143.

_____

_____

_____

_____

_____

_____

Name_____

 **SPELLING PRACTICE**

Blends

We are going to work with words that have the blends *spr*, *shr*, *str*, *squ*, *scr*, *spl*, and *thr*.

Learn to spell these words:

> scramble, scrape, shrimp, shrug, split, splurge, sprain, sprout, square, squat, strain, strip, thread, throat

Fill in the blanks using the spelling words. Each word is only used once.

(1) I hurt my ankle. I have a _____.

(2) I cough to clear my _____.

(3) I _____ when I lift my shoulders up and down.

(4) The little _____ are cute swimming in the ocean.

(5) I don't like to _____ my knee when I fall.

(6) I sew with a needle and _____.

(7) Would you like to _____ a piece of cake with me?

(8) A shape with four equal sides and four corners is called a _____.

(9) I am careful when I _____ down not to _____ my back.

(10) I see a _____ coming from the seed I planted.

(11) Sometimes I like to _____ and buy a large ice cream cone.

(12) We had to _____ the old paint off the wall before we could paint.

(13) I like to _____ my eggs before I cook them.

Write a fun sentence using at least two of your spelling words.

_____

_____

Write another fun sentence using two more of your spelling words.

_____

_____

Be sure to start each sentence with a capital letter and end it with a punctuation mark.

For More Practice:

Write your words in the shape boxes using the worksheet for this lesson available as a free download at masterbooks.com/classroom-aids.

Write your spelling words on notecards. Write one word on each card. You may create right-brain flashcards with your words.

Ask your teacher to read each spelling word. Spell the word out loud and use it in a sentence.

CREATE YOUR OWN DICTIONARY!

The Fieldmouse

By Cecil Frances Alexander

Where the acorn tumbles down,
Where the ash tree sheds its berry,
With your fur so soft and brown,
With your eye so round and merry,
Scarcely moving the long grass,
Fieldmouse, I can see you pass.

Little thing, in what dark den,
Lie you all the winter sleeping?
Till warm weather comes again,
Then once more I see you peeping
Round about the tall tree roots,
Nibbling at their fallen fruits.

Fieldmouse, fieldmouse, do not go,
Where the farmer stacks his treasure,
Find the nut that falls below,
Eat the acorn at your pleasure,
But you must not steal the grain
He has stacked with so much pain.

Make your hole where mosses spring,
Underneath the tall oak's shadow,
Pretty, quiet harmless thing,
Play about the sunny meadow.
Keep away from corn and house,
None will harm you, little mouse.

Comprehension

Were there any words you didn't understand? Circle them.

TEACHER NOTE

- The teacher should go over with the student the meaning of the circled words in the context of the poem.

NARRATION PRACTICE

(1) What is the title of the poem?

(2) Who is the author?

(3) What is this poem about?

(4) Each section of the poem is called a stanza. There are four stanzas in this poem. Which stanza is your favorite? Why?

Alexander, Cecil Frances. (1880) *Moral Songs.* London: Masters & Co., pp. 77-78.

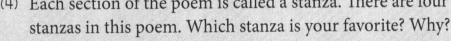

(5) Explain how this poem makes you feel.

Memorization

Memorize at least one stanza of this poem with your teacher.

TEACHER NOTE • Both the teacher and the student should work together to memorize the stanza.

Write a Poem

Write a poem with four lines. Every other line should rhyme. (**Hint:** Study the first four lines of each stanza of the poem you read. This type of poem has the ABAB pattern.)

_____

_____

_____

_____

INDEPENDENT READING

GRAMMAR PRACTICE

Nouns-Prefix, Root Word, Suffix

Do you remember what a prefix is? A **prefix** is letters added to the beginning of a word to change the meaning.

Match the prefix with the correct definition. (**Hint:** You will use one definition twice.)

(1)	bi-	bad or wrong
(2)	non-	too much, above
(3)	oct-	three
(4)	quad-	not
(5)	under-	eight
(6)	de-	four
(7)	mis-	too little, below
(8)	over-	two
(9)	tri-	reduce, remove, get off from, or do the opposite of

Do you remember what a suffix is? A **suffix** is letters added to the end of a word to change the meaning.

Match the suffix with the correct definition. (**Hint:** You will use two definitions twice.)

(10)	-al	
(11)	-en	act, result, or state of
(12)	-er	act, process
(13)	-ial	related to, character of
(14)	-ness	become, made of, resemble, to make
(15)	-ment	one who, that which
(16)	-or	condition, state of
(17)	-tion	

Do you remember what a root word is? The words we add a suffix or a prefix to is called a **root word**.

Match the root word with the correct definition.

(18) rupt   earth, ground, or soil

(19) terr   break or burst

(20) geo   measure

(21) photo   land

(22) tract   light

(23) meter or metr   pull or drag

JUST **4** FUN! **Word Scramble!**

See how many real words you can make by adding the prefixes and suffixes to the root words below. If you aren't sure, see what it looks like when you write it out. Remember to double check your word in a dictionary to make sure it is a real word!

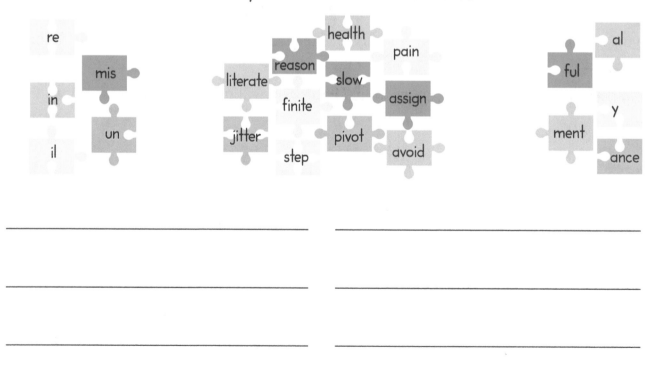

_____   _____

_____   _____

_____   _____

_____   _____

Review: Titles, Abbreviations

When you write a sentence using the title of a book, magazine, movie, or play, you should:

- Underline the title (or use italics if you are using a computer)
- Capitalize the first and last word
- Capitalize all other words except small words that are not nouns, verbs, or adjectives, such as: *the, for, and*

Write a sentence using the title of a book, movie, or play.

_____

_____

Do you remember what abbreviation means? It means to shorten. We can abbreviate names, titles, states, and postal codes.

Write the name of your state, the abbreviation, and the postal code.

(1) State Name: _____

(2) Abbreviation: _____ (3) Postal Code: _____

Write the abbreviation for each title.

(4) Mister _____ (7) Junior _____

(5) Miss _____ (8) Senior _____

(6) Missus _____

Draw a line from the name of each street to the correct abbreviation:

(9) Boulevard   Tpke.

(10) Highway   Blvd.

(11) Turnpike   Hwy.

READING
COMPREHENSION

Read "Jesus Cancels a Funeral" on pages 144–145 of *101 Favorite Stories from the Bible* with your teacher.

Answer the questions on page 145.

Copy Lamentations 3:32, then memorize it with your teacher.

_____

_____

_____

_____

Copy the picture on page 145. Color your picture.

Copy the caption from page 145.

_____

_____

_____

_____

_____

_____

B A C SPELLING PRACTICE

/f/ Sound Words

We are going to work with words that make the /f/ sound that use the letters *f*, *gh*, and *ph*.

Learn to spell these words:

> awful, elephant, enough, forever, fossil, freedom, gopher, graph, laugh, nephew, phone, phrase, physical, rough

The /f/ sound words heard about all those other letters going on a trip. They decided they needed to go too! Help them pack by putting each word in the correct suitcase.

(1) -gh words

(2) -ph words

(3) -f words

Write a fun sentence using at least two of your -f spelling words.

_____

_____

Write a fun sentence using at least two of your -gh spelling words.

_____

_____

Write a fun sentence using at least two of your -ph spelling words.

_____

_____

Be sure to start each sentence with a capital letter and end it with a punctuation mark.

For More Practice:

Write your words in the shape boxes using the worksheet for this lesson available as a free download at masterbooks.com/classroom-aids.

Write your spelling words on notecards. Write one word on each card. You may create right-brain flashcards with your words.

Ask your teacher to read each spelling word. Spell the word out loud and use it in a sentence.

CREATE YOUR OWN DICTIONARY!

The Spring Holy Days

Gathering the class around the Temple model, Mr. C. began, "The first spring holy day, Passover, took place long before the Temple was built in Jerusalem." He asked the class if they had studied Moses and the Exodus. Claire raised her hand and said, "Mr. Lopez talked about the plagues God sent upon the Egyptians and how the last plague was the angel of death. God's people killed a spotless lamb and put the blood on their doorposts. The angel passed over their homes. In Egypt, the angel killed all the first born. It was a very sad day, but the Pharaoh finally let the Israelites go free!"

Mr. C. thanked Claire, then explained that, for many years, people came to the Temple to celebrate Passover. "Jesus also came to the Temple for Passover, but He was about to become the Passover Lamb. He would lay His life down for us so that we can be forgiven by God. We are saved from our sins because of what Jesus did for us!" Then Mr. C. read from Romans chapter 10. Claire gave a thankful smile as he read verse 9, "that if you confess with your mouth Jesus as Lord, and believe in your heart that God raised Him from the dead, you will be saved."

Mr. C. continued, "God gave a way to be saved, but He also sent us the Holy Spirit to help us. The Saturday Sabbath, after Passover, He called The Feast of Firstfruits. From that day, the Israelites were to count 50 days in anticipation. Jesus' disciples had counted the 50 days when the Holy Spirit came upon them in the upper room! This day is called Pentecost. God is so loving and generous!"

NARRATION PRACTICE

(1) Where did the class gather?

(2) What did Claire say about the time of Moses and the Exodus?

(3) What did Mr. C. say about Jesus and the Passover?

(4) What does Romans 10:9 have to say about being saved?

(5) What did Mr. C. say about Pentecost?

TEACHER NOTE

- You may want to read with your students about the feasts in Leviticus 23. The full story of the Exodus is found in chapters 1–13. The tenth plague and the Passover begin at chapter 11. The accounts of the Crucifixion and Resurrection of Jesus can be found in Matthew 26–28, Mark 14–16, Luke 22–24, and John 18–20. The coming of the Holy Spirit is found in Acts 1–2. Please use discretion when covering difficult topics with your students.

Maps - Figure It Out!

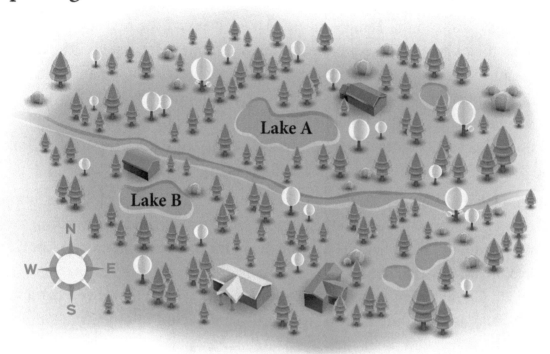

See if you can give your teacher answers to the following questions:

(1) Which house is closest to Lake A?

(2) Which house has two ponds near it?

(3) Which house is between the orange house and Lake B?

(4) Which house is closest to the river?

(5) How many ponds are on the map?

INDEPENDENT READING

 **GRAMMAR PRACTICE**

Review: Verbs

Do you remember what an action verb is? It tells what is happening in a sentence. Action verbs bring our sentences to life.

Write down two action verbs.

_____   _____

Write a sentence using the first action verb.

_____

_____

Write the same sentence using the second action verb.

_____

_____

Do you remember the eight **state of being verbs**? They are:

is   am   are   was   were   be   been   being

State of being verbs show state of being rather than action. They link the subject to the predicate.

Write a sentence using one of the state of being verbs.

_____

_____

There is another type of verb called **helping verbs**. Helping verbs help another verb in a sentence. They come before the main verb.

Study the helping verbs:

has	have	had	do	does	did
can	will	shall	could	would	should
must	may	might			

Write a sentence using a helping verb.

_____

_____

Study this example of a helping verb in a sentence:

Micah will bring Jin to his class.

The helping verb is _will_. The verb it helps is _bring_. Together, the helping verb and verb _will bring_ show us what is happening in the sentence. They make a great team!

The eight state of being verbs we learned can be helping verbs too! They also can be used with another verb to link the subject with the predicate. Here is an example:

Micah is bringing Jin to his class.

We changed our sentence just by changing the helping verb and verb team. We used one of our eight state of being verbs as a helping verb. The helping verb _is_ works with the verb _bringing_ to link the subject and predicate.

Now it is your turn! Write a sentence using one of the eight state of being verbs as a helping verb.

_____

_____

We have learned about action verbs, state of being verbs (which are sometimes helping verbs), and helping verbs. We learned about one more kind of verb, **linking verbs**.

Linking verbs link a noun or adjective to the subject of the sentence. When state of being verbs aren't acting like helping verbs, they are a linking verb. Here are some examples to study.

State of being helping verb:

I am driving to the store.

The word *am* is the state of being verb. The word *driving* is the main verb it is helping.

State of being linking verb:

Micah and Jin are good friends.

In this sentence, the state of being verb *are* links the subject *Micah and Jin* to the predicate *good friends*.

Tell whether the state of being verb is used as a helping verb or linking verb.

If it is a helping verb, write **H** after the sentence.

If it is a linking verb, write **L** after the sentence. (**Hint:** Remember, helping verbs help the main verb in a sentence.)

(1) Micah is writing in his journal. _____

(2) The Temple was huge. _____

(3) Micah and Claire were running to class. _____

(4) Micah and Claire are best friends. _____

Review: Simile

A *figure of speech* describes something in a way that is not literal. The meaning is not exactly what is written. It is figurative.

A *simile* is a figure of speech. It compares two different things using the words *like* or *as*.

We can make our sentences fun by using similes.

Write a sentence using the simile **as.**

_____

_____

Write a sentence using the simile **like.**

_____

_____

A *metaphor* is also a figure of speech. It compares two different things without using the words *like* or *as*.

My dog is a chicken.

Now it is your turn. Write a sentence using a fun metaphor. Remember, you can't use the words *like* or *as*.

_____

_____

JUST **4** FUN!

Which Goes Where ?

There are so many water pipes it's hard to tell which tap and line goes to what object. See if you can follow the pipes from the taps and figure out which goes where. Use the letters for the answers.

(1) Tap 1 goes to

_____ .

(2) Tap 2 goes to

_____ .

(3) Tap 3 goes to

_____ .

(4) Tap 4 goes to

_____ .

(5) Tap 5 goes to

_____ .

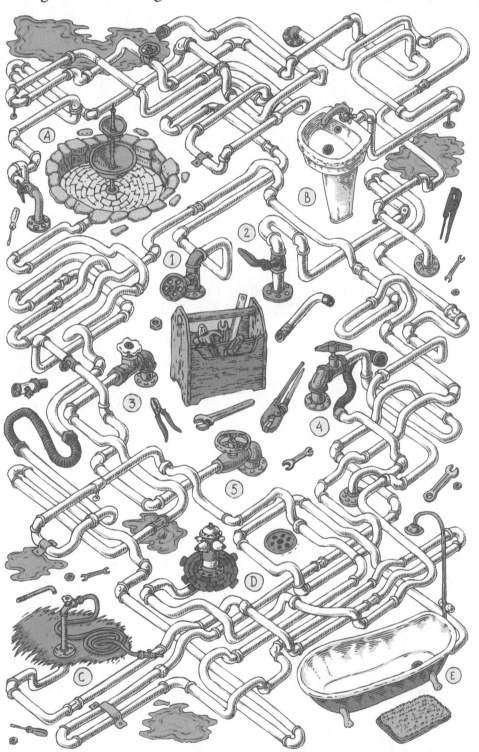

READING COMPREHENSION

Read "Miracle of the Fishes" on pages 146–147 of *101 Favorite Stories from the Bible* with your teacher.

Answer the questions on page 147.

Copy Mark 16:15b, then memorize it with your teacher.

_____

_____

_____

_____

Copy the picture on page 147. Color your picture.

Copy the caption from page 147.

_____

_____

_____

_____

_____

_____

SPELLING PRACTICE

/k/ and /qu/ Sound Words

We are going to work with words that make the /k/ and /qu/ sound. The /k/ sound can be spelled with the letters *c*, *k*, *ch*, and *ck*. Some words use -qu to make the /qu/ sound. Remember, the letter *q* is never found alone. It always travels with the letter *u*.

Learn to spell these words:

> anchor, chorus, circus, create, curious, kangaroo, kayak,
> napkin, nickel, pocket, quality, quiet, snack, squid

The *f* sound words didn't want to travel alone, so they invited the /k/ and /qu/ sound words to join them on their trip. Now the /k/ and /qu/ sound words need to pack too! Help them get ready by putting each word in the correct suitcase.

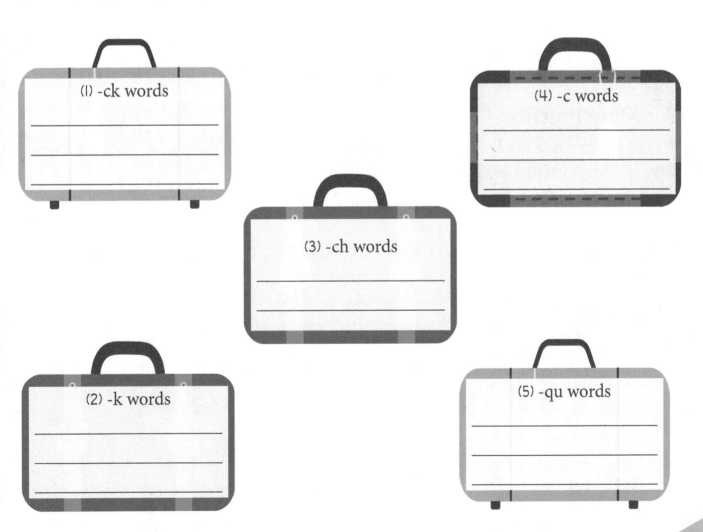

(1) -ck words

(4) -c words

(3) -ch words

(2) -k words

(5) -qu words

Write a fun sentence using at least two of your /k/ sound spelling words.

_____

_____

Write a fun sentence using two more of your /k/ sound spelling words.

_____

_____

Write a fun sentence using at least two of your /qu/ sound spelling words.

_____

_____

Be sure to start each sentence with a capital letter and end it with a punctuation mark.

For More Practice:

Write your words in the shape boxes using the worksheet for this lesson available as a free download at masterbooks.com/classroom-aids.

Write your spelling words on notecards. Write one word on each card. You may create right-brain flashcards with your words.

Ask your teacher to read each spelling word. Spell the word out loud and use it in a sentence.

CREATE YOUR OWN DICTIONARY!

Title: Children Fishing

Artist: Illarion Mikhailovich Pryanishnikov

OBSERVATION SKILLS

(1) What is the name of this painting?

(2) What is happening in this painting?

(3) Describe the people in this painting.

(4) Describe where this picture takes place.

(5) What colors are used in this picture?

(6) How does this picture make you feel? Why?

Story Writing

Finish this story about the picture. Use at least three sentences.

It was bright and early, but the children couldn't wait to go fishing!

_____

_____

_____

_____

_____

_____

_____

INDEPENDENT READING

 **GRAMMAR PRACTICE**

Review: Verbs

A verb can tell us whether the sentence takes place in the past, present, or future. We call this **verb tense**.

Let's see how we can use the verb *run* to show action in the past, present, and future. (**Hint:** The future tense uses the helping verb *will* or *shall*.)

I ran fast. (Past)

I run fast. (Present)

I will run fast. (Future)

Sometimes we can add the suffix *-ed* or *-d* to a verb to show it happened in the past. Study the example:

Claire called Micah over to her table.

Sometimes we can add the suffix *-ing* to a verb to show it is happening in the present. (**Hint:** Sometimes when *-ing* is added to a verb, the present tense uses a helping verb before the main verb.)

Study the example:

Micah is eating a fig cake.

For each verb, write a sentence in the past, present, and future. (**Hint:** You may need to change the verb. You may also need to use a helping verb.)

Write past, present, or future next to each sentence.

(1) Claire will bake fig cakes. _____

(2) Claire baked Micah a fig cake. _____

(3) Claire is baking a fig cake. _____

Do you remember our helping verbs? You may look back if you need to. Remember, state of being verbs can be helping verbs.

A **phrase** is a small group of words. A **helping verb phrase** is a small group of helping verbs. There are many helping verb phrases. Some examples include:

can be	could be	may be	might be
has been	have been	had been	might have been

Here is a helping verb phrase used in a sentence:

Micah could be eating a fig cake.

A **verb phrase** is a helping verb (or helping verb phrase) and the main verb. Look at the sentence again.

(4)   What is the verb phrase? _____

Write a sentence using a verb phrase.

_____

_____

When we write a sentence, the subject and the linking verb must agree.

How do we make sure our subject and linking verb agree?

- First, we look at our subject. Is it singular or plural? (**Hint:** Singular means one. Plural means more than one.)
- Then we look at our linking verb. Is it present or past tense?
- Check the chart to make sure we used the right linking verb for our subject.

Let's study the chart:

Verb Agreement		
Subject	Present Tense	Past Tense
Singular: he, she, it	is	was
Plural: we, they, you	are	were
I	am	was

Draw a line to the correct linking verb for each sentence.

(5) They _____ at church. (present)   are

(6) They _____ at church. (past)   were

Write a sentence using a singular subject and a present tense linking verb.

_____

_____

Review: Dictionary, Thesaurus

 **TEACHER NOTE** • The student will need a dictionary for this lesson. A children's dictionary is recommended.

Ask your teacher for a dictionary. Open the dictionary to any page. You will see two words at the top of the page, usually one on each side. These are called *guide words*. They tell you the first and last words that are found on the page.

Now, look at the words with definitions listed on the page of your dictionary. They are in alphabetical order. The first word is the first guide word. The last word is the last guide word. Guide words make it easier to look up words in the dictionary.

Open your dictionary to any page. Write the guide words:

_____   _____

Write any three words found on the page in alphabetical order:

_____

_____

_____

A dictionary can show us how to say a word. Look up the word *chase* in your dictionary. Right after the word, it shows you how to say the word. The phonics markings show how to say the vowel. My dictionary shows it like this:

chase (chās)

Look up these words in your dictionary. How fast can you find them? Copy how to say each word.

(1) sail _____

(2) ship _____

Do you remember what synonyms and antonyms are?

> Synonyms are two words that mean the same thing.

> Antonyms are two words that have opposite meanings.

Write a synonym and antonym for each word:

fast: _____   _____

real: _____   _____

A **thesaurus** is a book of synonyms and antonyms. We can use a thesaurus to help us find the best words to use in our writing.

Ask your teacher for a thesaurus. Find in the thesaurus the word: **drag.**

Write a synonym and an antonym for the word drag.

_____   _____

Write a sentence using a synonym for the word drag.

_____

_____

Write a sentence using an antonym for the word drag.

_____

_____

READING COMPREHENSION

Read "Jairus' Daughter and a Desperate Woman" on pages 148–149 of *101 Favorite Stories from the Bible* with your teacher.

Answer the questions on page 149.

Copy John 11:45, then memorize it with your teacher.

_____

_____

_____

_____

Copy the picture on page 149. Color your picture.

Copy the caption from page 149.

_____

_____

_____

_____

_____

_____

Silent Letter Words

We are going to work with words that have silent letters.

Learn to spell these words:

> answer, calf, design, gnaw, honor, hymn, knife,
> knight, listen, plumber, sword, thumb, wheeze, wrench

Find the spelling words in the word search.

- o answer
- o calf
- o design
- o gnaw
- o honor
- o hymn
- o knight
- o knife
- o listen
- o plumber
- o sword
- o thumb
- o wheeze
- o wrench

```
X N M Q Z L I I A O J H Y M N
F Q X D F G I F Q H S Z S H M
F H M G E A M S P L V H R Y V
R C A L F M J F T E H C H G C
D K G R H U K W J E O P R M A
U N I P L U M B E R N E L V M
L I V W P U G G E P O H T G Q
M F F H H J C W E Q R Z H P B
G E L E L U S K N I G H T M I
N L O E W N K J C J E P U D K
A O W Z A E U N X X K H R D W
W F D E S I G N Z C T P R P S
B E P I W R E N C H B O Y H V
H Y F K P T L Q V Q W U N A I
R A M F K L N W T S X W M F P
```

Write a fun sentence using at least two of your spelling words.

_____

_____

Write another fun sentence using at least two more of your spelling words.

_____

_____

Be sure to start each sentence with a capital letter and end it with a punctuation mark.

For More Practice:

Write your words in the shape boxes using the worksheet for this lesson available as a free download at masterbooks.com/classroom-aids.

Write your spelling words on notecards. Write one word on each card. You may create right-brain flashcards with your words.

Ask your teacher to read each spelling word. Spell the word out loud and use it in a sentence.

CREATE YOUR OWN DICTIONARY!

Mr. Clark's Visit

As Micah went into his class, Mrs. Clark's husband greeted him! Micah was excited as Mr. C. introduced Mr. Clark as their special guest, a missionary to Honduras. He didn't have to wait long to see if there were pictures from Honduras. Mr. Clark set a stack of photos on Mr. C.'s desk while inviting the children up.

Micah looked eagerly for pictures of Carlos and his little brother, Diego. Claire pointed one out. Wow! They sure had grown! He barely recognized them. Carlos looked so big and strong as he carried Diego on his shoulders. Micah wondered if Jin had seen this picture of their two pen pals. Micah soon got lost in his thoughts of Honduras. He jumped when Ava shoved a white envelope into his hand. Micah tore it open and began to read.

> May 1, 2021
>
> Dear Micah,
>
> We have had a busy year planting fruit trees. I love to help take care of them. Soon we will have plenty of fresh fruit for all of us! Please thank everyone at your church for helping us with this project. It has meant so much to us.
>
> When I am not helping with the trees or playing with Diego, I can usually be found studying. My school work isn't too hard, but sometimes I daydream about bananas, oranges, papaya, and lichas. I forget I am supposed to be solving math problems and learning about verbs!
>
> I hope you are doing well.
>
> Your Friend,
> Carlos

When class was over, Micah couldn't wait to show Jin his letter. He also hoped Jin could help him figure out what lichas are!

 **NARRATION PRACTICE**

(1) Who greeted Micah when he entered the class?

(2) Describe the photo Micah saw.

(3) What did Carlos say in his letter to Micah?

(4) Do you know what lichas are?

 **TEACHER NOTE**

- You may want to research with your students lichas and other fruit trees that grow in Honduras.

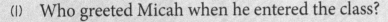

Grouping

Write a word that belongs to each group.

(1) soccer   football   basketball   _____

(2) cow   chicken   goat   _____

(3) boots   sandals   socks   _____

(4) whale   dolphin   starfish   _____

INDEPENDENT READING

GRAMMAR PRACTICE

Review: Adjectives, Adverbs

Do you remember what an adjective is? An *adjective* describes a noun. Do you remember what a noun is? It is a person, place, or thing. An adjective describes a person, place, or thing.

An adjective can describe:

color, size, shape	tastes, smells, sounds
how many, looks, feels	weather, feelings, behavior

Write a sentence using at least two adjectives.

_____

_____

Do you remember what an article is? An *article* comes before a noun. There are three articles: *a, an, the.* Articles are a type of adjective.

Remember:

> Articles come before a noun and are a type of adjective.
> Use *a* before words that start with a consonant.
> Use *an* before words that start with a vowel.
> Use *the* to refer to a specific noun.

Write a sentence using at least two articles:

_____

_____

Adverbs are similar to adjectives, but instead of describing a noun, they describe a verb. Adverbs often end in *ly* and describe *how, when, where,* or *how often* a verb happens.

There are many adverbs. Here is a list of examples to study:

How	When	Where	How Often
gently	early	above	daily
quickly	now	inside	never
quietly	soon	here	often
sadly	tomorrow	outside	usually
safely	yesterday	upstairs	yearly

For each sentence, find the adverb and draw an arrow to the verb it describes:

(1) Claire quickly climbed the tree.

(2) Micah never eats pumpkin pie.

Write a sentence using an adverb that tells *how* or *when*:

_____

_____

Write a sentence using an adverb that tells *where* or *how often*:

_____

_____

Review: Parts of a Story

Do you remember the parts of a story?

A story has a *title*. The title is the name of a book.

A story has an *author*. The author is who wrote the book.

A story has *characters*. Characters are the people or animals in the story.

The *setting* is where and when a story takes place. The setting can be a small place like a kitchen or a big place like a town. A story can take place long ago or just yesterday.

The *plot* is what happens in the story. It tells us what the conflict or the problem is, what happens, and how the conflict or problem is solved. It has a beginning, middle, and end.

The *conclusion*, or ending, answers any questions that need to be answered and wraps up the story.

We can think of a story like a train. It has lots of cars, but it makes up one train.

Match the parts of a story with what they are:

(1) conclusion   ending

(2) author   problem: beginning, middle, end

(3) characters   where and when

(4) setting   who

(5) plot   the person who wrote it

Read "Bartimaeus Cries Out" on pages 150–151 of *101 Favorite Stories from the Bible* with your teacher.

Answer the questions on page 151.

Copy Isaiah 35:5, then memorize it with your teacher.

_____

_____

_____

_____

Copy the picture on page 151. Color your picture.

Copy the caption from page 151.

_____

_____

_____

_____

_____

_____

SPELLING PRACTICE

Double Consonant Words

We are going to work with words that have double consonants.

Learn to spell these words:

> suffer, shuffle, collar, valley, cattle, mitten, squirrel,
> mirror, riddle, giggle, pepper, rabbit, tunnel, essay

Write your spelling words in alphabetical order.

(1) _____   (8) _____

(2) _____   (9) _____

(3) _____   (10) _____

(4) _____   (11) _____

(5) _____   (12) _____

(6) _____   (13) _____

(7) _____   (14) _____

Write a fun sentence using at least two of your spelling words.

_____

_____

Write another fun sentence using at least two more of your spelling words.

_____

_____

Be sure to start each sentence with a capital letter and end it with a punctuation mark.

For More Practice:

Write your words in the shape boxes using the worksheet for this lesson available as a free download at masterbooks.com/classroom-aids.

Write your spelling words on notecards. Write one word on each card. You may create right-brain flashcards with your words.

Ask your teacher to read each spelling word. Spell the word out loud and use it in a sentence.

 CREATE YOUR OWN DICTIONARY!

Psalm 117

[1]Praise the LORD, all nations;

Laud Him, all peoples!

[2]For His lovingkindness is great toward us,

And the truth of the LORD is everlasting.

Praise the LORD!

Comprehension

Were there any words you didn't understand? Circle them.

 **TEACHER NOTE**

• The teacher should go over with the student the meaning of the circled words in the context of the psalm.

 **NARRATION PRACTICE**

(1) What chapter of Psalms did you read?

(2) How many verses are there in this chapter? Did this surprise you?

(3) What is this psalm about?

(4) What did you learn about God in this psalm?

(5) Why do you think this psalm is so short?

Memorization

Memorize Psalm 117 with your teacher.

Write a Psalm

Write a psalm that has at least two verses. Each verse should have at least two lines. Remember, a psalm is a song. It praises God. After you write your psalm, think of a tune and sing it!

_____

_____

_____

_____

_____

_____

INDEPENDENT READING

 **GRAMMAR PRACTICE**

Review:
Homonyms, Homophones, Homographs

Do you remember the differences between homophones, homonyms, and homographs?

Let's study the charts:

Homophones	Homonyms	Homographs
· sound the same · different meanings · spelled differently	· sound the same · different meanings · spelled the same	· sound differently · different meanings · spelled the same
Example: hair – hare	Example: pen – pen	Example: bass – bass

(1)   What is the same about homophones, homonyms, and homographs? (**Hint:** Look at the middle section of each one.)

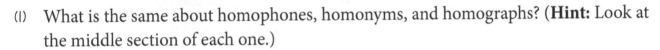

_____

Match homophones, homonyms, and homographs to the correct descriptions. (**Hint:** You won't use one of the answers.)

(1) homophones
(2) homographs
(3) homonyms

sound the same
different sound
same meanings
different meaning
same spelling
different spelling

Review: Writing a Letter

Last week Micah read a letter from Carlos. Study the letter below. The main part of his letter is called the body.

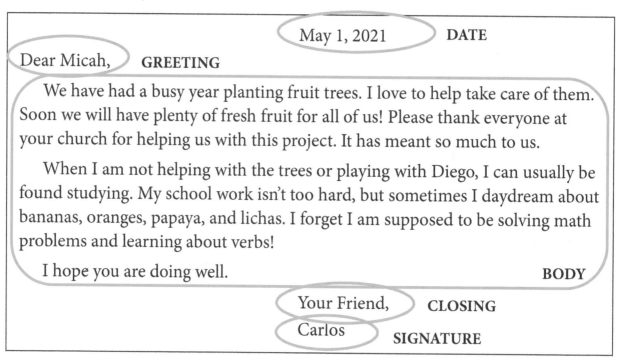

May 1, 2021   **DATE**

Dear Micah,   **GREETING**

    We have had a busy year planting fruit trees. I love to help take care of them. Soon we will have plenty of fresh fruit for all of us! Please thank everyone at your church for helping us with this project. It has meant so much to us.

    When I am not helping with the trees or playing with Diego, I can usually be found studying. My school work isn't too hard, but sometimes I daydream about bananas, oranges, papaya, and lichas. I forget I am supposed to be solving math problems and learning about verbs!

    I hope you are doing well.   **BODY**

Your Friend,   **CLOSING**

Carlos   **SIGNATURE**

Write a letter to a friend or relative. You may want to tell them about some things you like to do, just like Carlos did.

Ask your teacher for paper and an envelope for your letter.

Be sure to put the parts of your letter in the correct place:

    ○ date

    ○ greeting

    ○ body

    ○ closing

    ○ signature

When you write the body of your letter, remember to use what you learned about writing paragraphs.

Check off each part as you write your paragraph:

    ○ Write the topic sentence. Remember to indent your topic sentence.

    ○ Write 2–3 sentences that give details about your topic.

    ○ Write a concluding sentence.

Be sure to:

    ○ Correctly capitalize your words

    ○ Use correct punctuation

Now it is time to put the address on your envelope and mail it!

When you address an envelope, be sure to put each address in the correct place. An address includes:

    ○ First and last name

    ○ House number and street name

    ○ City, state abbreviation, and zip code

Follow the example for writing addresses on an envelope. Ask your teacher for help.

READING COMPREHENSION

Read "A Paralyzed Man" on pages 152–153 of *101 Favorite Stories from the Bible* with your teacher.

Answer the questions on page 153.

Copy Mark 9:23, then memorize it with your teacher.

_____

_____

_____

_____

Copy the picture on page 153. Color your picture.

Copy the caption from page 153.

_____

_____

_____

_____

_____

 **SPELLING PRACTICE**

Ordinal Number Words 1–10

We are going to work with ordinal number words. Ordinal numbers show place. If you are the eleventh person in line, you are in the eleventh place.

TEACHER NOTE
- The teacher may want to spend some time talking about ordinal numbers.

Learn to spell these words:

> eleventh, twelfth, thirteenth, fourteenth, fifteenth, sixteenth, seventeenth, eighteenth, nineteenth, twentieth, twenty-first, twenty-second, twenty-third, twenty-fourth

Write the ordinal numbers.

(1) 11 _____

(2) 12 _____

(3) 13 _____

(4) 14 _____

(5) 15 _____

(6) 16 _____

(7) 17 _____

(8) 18 _____

(9) 19 _____

(10) 20 _____

(11) 21 _____

(12) 22 _____

(13) 23 _____

(14) 24 _____

Write a fun sentence using at least one of your spelling words.

_____

_____

For More Practice:

Write your words in the shape boxes using the worksheet for this lesson available as a free download at masterbooks.com/classroom-aids.

Write your spelling words on notecards. Write one word on each card. You may create right-brain flashcards with your words.

Ask your teacher to read each spelling word. Spell the word out loud and use it in a sentence.

CREATE YOUR OWN DICTIONARY!

A Variety of Food

Micah and Claire were eagerly writing letters to their friends in Honduras. Micah told Carlos about all the places Mr. C. had been. He also told Carlos about the different foods Mr. C. had tried. Micah would not have tried some of them, but he was inspired to try new foods. He asked Carlos about lichas. He also asked Carlos what other foods they eat in Honduras. Micah was fascinated by how people eat differently, depending on where they live. He always thought everyone ate the same foods as his family! He realized there are more foods than he could have imagined.

All of this talk of food got Micah wondering. Do they prepare foods differently in other countries too? Do they have cook tops and ovens in Honduras? Do they cook with electricity or gas? All of these questions would have to wait because Mr. C. was about to dismiss the class. Just as Micah signed his name, Mr. C. asked Claire to collect the letters.

Mr. C. assured the students that Mr. Clark would deliver their letters as soon as he got back to Honduras. Micah was eager to have his questions answered about Honduran food, but it would be a long wait. The orphanage was in a remote area, so they had to rely on the Clarks to deliver the letters. Micah reminded himself that patience is a fruit of the Spirit. He chuckled to himself as he thought, *Hey, that is some food I probably need more of!*

NARRATION PRACTICE

(1) What did Micah write and ask Carlos about in his letter?

(2) When he thought of food, Micah was wondering about what kinds of questions?

(3) How was Micah's letter to Carlos going to be delivered?

(4) Micah reminded himself of which fruit of the Spirit?

Observation

Study the picture then write a paragraph, telling a story about the picture. Be sure to use ideas from the picture for your story.

You may want to think about these questions before you start to write:

○ Where does the picture take place?

○ Who is in the picture?

○ What are they doing?

○ What else do you see in the picture?

○ What else do you notice about the picture?

Check off each part as you write your paragraph:

○ Write the topic sentence. Remember to indent your topic sentence.

○ Write 2–3 sentences that give details about your topic.

○ Write a concluding sentence.

_____

_____

_____

_____

_____

_____

_____

INDEPENDENT READING

Fourth Quarter Review (Each question is 4 points) Students may use the study sheets in the back of the book.

Write a proper noun for each common noun.

(1) holiday _____

Write the possessive noun for each noun:

(2) mom _____   (3) moms _____

Make each noun plural by adding *s* or *es*:

(4) chimney _____   (6) radio _____

(5) church _____

Change these words to make them plural:

(7) half _____   (8) bakery _____

Match the singular nouns with the correct plural noun.

(9) goose   oxen

(10) mouse   mice

(11) ox   geese

In the sentence below, underline the prepositional phrase, then circle the preposition. Finally, write **OP** above the object of the preposition.

(12) Micah went into his room.

(13) Write a sentence using a quotation.

_____

_____

Match the prefix, suffix, and root words with the correct definition.

(14) **quad-**   one who, that which

(15) **-al or -ial**   four

(16) **-er or -or**   earth, ground, or soil

(17) **geo**   related to, character of

Tell whether the state of being verb is used as a helping verb or linking verb.

If it is a helping verb, write **H** after the sentence.

If it is a linking verb, write **L** after the sentence. (**Hint:** Remember, helping verbs help the main verb in a sentence.)

(18) **Micah and Claire were running to class.** _____

(19) **Micah and Claire are best friends.** _____

(20) Write a sentence using the past tense.

_____

_____

(21) Write a sentence using at least two adjectives.

_____

_____

(22) Write a sentence using an adverb.

_____

_____

Match homophones, homonyms, and homographs to the correct descriptions. (**Hint:** You won't use one of the answers.)

sound the same

different sound

(23) homophones

(24) homographs

(25) homonyms

same meanings

different meaning

same spelling

different spelling

 JUST **4** FUN!

Lost Letters!

Claire and Micah's letters to Honduras were being hand-delivered. If you write a letter to someone, it usually goes to the post office for delivery. See if you can find the words below in the puzzle grid. Circle or highlight the words as you find them.

parcel

postman

post box

stamp

envelope

letter

box

post office

Fourth Quarter Review (Each question is 4 points) Students may use the study sheets in the back of the book.

What kind of sentences are these?

Put an **IM** for imperative, **D** for declarative, **E** for exclamatory, and **IN** for interrogative:

(1) _____ Why did the students make flashcards?

(2) _____ I like to memorize the books of the Bible.

(3) _____ God is good!

(4) _____ Get out your Bible.

Put commas in the right place in each sentence. (**Hint:** Some sentences have more than one comma.)

(5) Did Claire make the flashcards Micah?

(6) Micah washed the dishes folded his clothes and made his bed.

(7) Ava did you eat popcorn?

(8) How long Jin did it take to memorize the books of the Bible?

(9) Write a sentence using an interjection.

_____

_____

(10) Underline the subject and circle the predicate of the sentence.

Micah wanted Jin in his class.

(II) Combine the two sentences using a conjunction.

I like apples.
I love peaches.

_____

_____

(12) Write a sentence using the title of a book, movie, or play.

_____

_____

Draw a line from the name of each street to the correct abbreviation:

(13) Boulevard   Blvd.
(14) Highway   Tpke.
(15) Turnpike   Hwy.

(16) Write a sentence using the simile like.

_____

_____

(17) Write a sentence using the simile as.

_____

_____

(18) Write a sentence using a metaphor.

_____

_____

Write a synonym and antonym for each word:

(19) **happy:** _____   _____

(20) **clean:** _____   _____

Match the parts of a story with what they are:

(21) **conclusion**   ending

(22) **author**   problem: beginning, middle, end

(23) **characters**   where and when

(24) **setting**   who

(25) **plot**   the person who wrote it

READING COMPREHENSION

Read "Five Loaves and Two Fishes" on pages 154–155 of *101 Favorite Stories from the Bible* with your teacher.

Answer the questions on page 155.

Copy Matthew 6:33, then memorize it with your teacher.

_____

_____

_____

_____

Copy the picture on page 155. Color your picture.

Copy the caption from page 155.

_____

_____

_____

_____

_____

_____

Spelling Review

Use your flashcards to practice your spelling words.

You may:

- Ask someone to quiz you on how to spell the words
- Play spelling games found in the back of the book
- Create your own spelling games
- Use each word in a sentence and say it to your teacher

 **CREATE YOUR OWN DICTIONARY!**

Students may choose their own words this week for their dictionary.

Teacher Aids

How to use this section

These pages are included for the teacher to provide to the student. The teacher may make copies of the practice pages, or they can be laminated (or put in page protectors) and used with dry erase markers.

Study sheets are for the student to use for reference and for further study as needed.

The activities and games are fun ideas to use with lessons or for extra practice.

Table of Contents:

Assessments

We have provided Quarterly Reviews within the curriculum at the end of each quarter. Each quarter has two reviews covering punctuation, grammar, and writing. There is also a spelling review. The reviews provided each quarter may be used as quizzes or tests for grading purposes. Students should be given access to the study sheets in the back of the book when completing the Quarterly Reviews.

Grading Options for This Course:

It is always the option of an educator to assess student grades however he or she might deem best. For *Language Lessons,* the teacher may evaluate whether a student has mastered a particular skill or whether the student needs additional experience. A teacher may rank these on a five-point scale as follows:

Skill Mastered				Needs Experience
5 (equals an A)	4 (B)	3 (C)	2 (D)	1 (equals an F)

A — Student shows complete mastery of concepts with no errors.

B — Student shows mastery of concepts with minimal errors.

C — Student shows partial mastery of concepts. Review of some concepts is needed.

D — Student shows minimal understanding of concepts. Review is needed.

F — Student does not show understanding of concepts. Review is needed.

First Semester Assessment Chart

	First Quarter	Skill Mastered	Needs Experience
Week 1	Analogy, Independent Reading		
	Nouns: people, places, things, Proper: I, holidays		
	Sentences: capitalization, punctuation, four types of sentences, complete sentences		
	a Words (break, drain, eight, flake, holiday, jail, past, shape, spam, stamp, steak, stray, talent, weigh); Dictionary		
Week 2	Sight Words, Independent Reading		
	Possessive, Plural Possessive Nouns		
	Sentences: combining, subject/predicate		
	e Words (desk, spent, been, meant, leather, speed, green, peach, east, chief, niece, alley, gently, squeeze); Dictionary		
Week 3	Maps/Directions, Sight Words Practice, Independent Reading		
	Plural Pronouns		
	Conjunctions, Interjections		
	i Words (align, build, deny, diet, flight, grind, height, inch, pilot, ruin, shine, sting, thigh, type); Dictionary		
Week 4	Memorize, Sight Words, Independent Reading		
	Possessive Pronouns		
	Sentences: subject-compound subject, Predicate-compound verb		
	o Words (broke, coast, crow, globe, goal, gold, growth, host, problem, shock, shop, shown, snow, wrote); Dictionary		
Week 5	Sequencing, Sight Words, Independent Reading		
	Verbs: action		
	Sentences: quotation marks		
	u Words (done, cute, fruit, glue, group, nephew, prove, punish, rescue, smooth, threw, truth, tube, unit); Dictionary		
Week 6	Story Writing, Independent Reading		
	State of Being Verbs, Helping Verbs		
	Commas: in a list, personal address		
	ow, aw Words (crawl, drawn, exalt, false, faucet, fault, frown, howl, launch, mount, pounce, sauce, sound, sprout); Dictionary		
Week 7	Observation: picture, Independent Reading		
	State of Being Verbs, Helping Verbs		
	Titles: books, magazines, movies, plays		
	aught, ought, ound Words (astound, bought, brought, caught, daughter, fought, found, fraught, ground, hound, ought, sought, taught, thought); Dictionary		
Week 8	Memorize, Syllables, Independent Reading		
	State of Being Verbs as Helping Verbs and Linking Verbs		
	Sentences: writing a paragraph		
	-ar, -or, -er, -ir, -ur Words (appear, board, career, course, dairy, declare, journey, learn, perhaps, purpose, score, sharp, twirl, worn); Dictionary		

		Skill Mastered	Needs Experience
Week 9	Rhyming: ABAB, Independent Reading		
	1st Quarter Review		
	1st Quarter Review		
	1st Quarter Spelling Review		
	*Second Quarter*		
Week 1	Maps/Directions, Independent Reading		
	Verb Tense: past, present, future		
	Dictionary: guide words, pronunciation key		
	Compound Words (railroad, pinecone, sunflower, fingernail, newspaper, wheelchair, fireplace, tailgate, homesick, bedroom, twenty-one, get-together, seat belt, ice cream); Dictionary		
Week 2	Story Writing, Independent Reading		
	Verb Phrase		
	Contractions		
	Contractions (can't, could've, didn't, don't, haven't, I'd, I'm, It's, I've, shouldn't, wasn't, won't, would've, you'd); Dictionary		
Week 3	Acronyms, Independent Reading		
	Verb Agreement		
	Abbreviations: states		
	plural -s, -es; + y, vowel + o, consonant + o, exceptions Words (fleas, themes, rocks, chimneys, rodeos, heroes, buses, fusses, wishes, churches, foxes, boxes, pianos, photos); Dictionary		
Week 4	Memorize, Rhyming, Independent Reading		
	Word Usage: verbs-see, saw, seen, real, really		
	Abbreviations: people, streets, initials, titles, Jr., Sr.		
	Plural f to v, y to i Words (calves, cliffs, countries, enemies, halves, ladies, leaves, lives, mysteries, roofs, supplies, twenties, wives, wolves); Dictionary		
Week 5	Story Writing, Independent Reading		
	Word Usage: verbs-eat, ate, eaten, go, went, gone		
	Synonyms, Antonyms, Thesaurus		
	Irregular Plural Words (cacti, children, corn, deer, fish, geese, mice, moose, octopi, oxen, people, seaweed, sheep, women); Dictionary		
Week 6	Story Writing, Independent Reading		
	Word Usage: this, that, these, those		
	Comparison -er, -est,		
	Suffixes -er and -est Words (closer, closest, funnier, funniest, greater, greatest, hotter, hottest, larger, largest, redder, reddest, taller, tallest); Dictionary		
Week 7	Word Categories, Short Story, Independent Reading		
	Word Usage: it's, its, who's, whose		
	Figures of Speech: simile, metaphor		
	-er, or, and -ar Words (answer, beggar, calendar, chapter, collar, director, doctor, labor, motor, polar, proper, sailor, sugar, weather); Dictionary		
Week 8	Write a Psalm, Memorizing, Independent Reading		
	Word Usage: most, almost, sit, set		
	Sentences: writing a paragraph		
	-el, -al, and -le Words (barrel, battle, candle, eagle, final, metal, model, nickel, pedal, simple, special, title, total, towel); Dictionary		

		Skill Mastered	Needs Experience
Week 9	Fact vs. Opinion, Independent Reading		
	2nd Quarter Review		
	2nd Quarter Review		
	2nd Quarter Spelling Review		

Second Semester Assessment Chart

	Third Quarter		
Week 1	Memorize Books of the Bible, Write a Story, Independent Reading		
	Adjectives: articles-a, an, the; What Kind? Which One? How Many? color, size, shape, taste, smells, sounds, looks, feels, weather, feeling, behavior		
	Prefix: non-, over-, mis-, de-, under-, bi-, tri-, quad-, oct-		
	Prefix non-, over-, mis-, de-, under-, bi-, tri-, quad-, oct- Words (bicycle, decrease, defeat, misbehave, misread, nonsense, octagon, octopus, overdone, overheard, quadrant, triangle, underground, understand); Dictionary		
Week 2	Rhyming, Independent Reading		
	Adverbs: how often, how, when, where		
	Suffix: -er, -or, -tion, -al, -ial, -ness, -ment, -en		
	Suffix -er, -or, -tion, -al, -ial, -ness, -ment, -en Words (actor, builder, colonial, conductor, creation, dental, enjoyment, farmer, illness, kindness, natural, partial, vacation, wooden); Dictionary		
Week 3	Memorize, Maps/Direction, Independent Reading		
	Prepositions: prepositional phrase, object of the preposition		
	Root Words: -rupt, terr, geo, photo, tract, meter, metr		
	Root Words -rupt, terr, geo, photo, tract, meter, metr (disrupt, erupt, geology, geography, metric, metronome, odometer, perimeter, photocopy, photograph, subtract, terrain, territory, traction); Dictionary		
Week 4	Memorize, Write a Poem, Independent Reading		
	Homonyms, Homophones		
	Sentences: writing a better sentence		
	Homophones (beat, beet, blew, blue, dear, deer, pain, pane, pray, prey, sail, sale, wait, weight); Dictionary		
Week 5	Memorize, Story Writing, Independent Reading		
	Homophones: to, too, two, there, their, they're		
	Sentences: writing a paragraph		
	Homonyms (fire, bark, foot, rock, iron, change, left, pound, bear, trunk, rose, squash, handle, organ); Dictionary		
Week 6	Story Writing, Independent Reading		
	Homographs		
	Parts of a Story: setting, character, plot, conclusion		
	Soft and Hard c and g Words (bounce, carrot, citizen, country, cymbals, damage, edge, gather, ginger, granted, gymnastics, include, since, yogurt); Dictionary		
Week 7	Memorize Books of the Bible, Fact or Opinion, Independent Reading		
	Eight Parts of Speech: nouns, verbs, pronouns, adjectives, adverbs, preposition, interjection, conjunction		
	Book Report: parts of a story-setting, character		
	-ie and -ei, -oy and -oi Words (believe, brief, boiler, ceiling, cowboy, destroy, exploit, receipt, retrieve, their, toilet, voyage, weigh, yield); Dictionary		

		Skill Mastered	Needs Experience
Week 8	Memorize, Write a Psalm, Independent Reading		
	Eight Parts of Speech: nouns, verbs, pronouns, adjectives, adverbs, preposition, interjection, conjunction		
	Book Report: parts of a story-plot, conclusion		
	Three-syllable Words (compromise, direction, suddenly, following, afternoon, holiday, family, behavior, alphabet, internet, navigate, document, remember, edible); Dictionary		
Week 9	Memorize, Independent Reading		
	3rd Quarter Review		
	3rd Quarter Review		
	3rd Quarter Spelling Review		
	Fourth Quarter		
Week 1	Memorization, Syllables, Independent Reading		
	Review: nouns-proper, pronouns, antecedent, possessive		
	Review: sentences-types, punctuation, commas, interjections		
	ng, nk, nt, pt, sc, sk, st Words (belong, bling, blanket, drink, frequent, saint, tempt, swept, scared, scope, skirt, skunk, starve, least); Dictionary		
Week 2	Comprehension, Independent Reading		
	Review: nouns-plural, irregular plural		
	Review: sentences-subject/predicate, compound subject, combining, conjunctions		
	sh, th, ch, -tch Words (sharpen, shape, brush, thirsty, thank, change, challenge, preach, attach, latch, stretch, watch, kitchen, chicken); Dictionary		
Week 3	Memorization, Independent Reading		
	Review: prepositions		
	Sentences: quotation marks		
	spr, shr, str, squ, scr, spl, thr Words (sprain, sprout, shrimp, shrug, strip, strain, square, squat, scramble, scrape, split, splurge, thread, throat); Dictionary		
Week 4	Memorization, Write a Poem, Independent Reading		
	Review: prefix, suffix, root words		
	Review: titles, abbreviations		
	f, gh, ph Words (awful, elephant, enough, forever, fossil, freedom, gopher, graph, laugh, nephew, phone, phrase, physical, rough); Dictionary		
Week 5	Maps/Directions, Independent Reading		
	Review: verbs-action, state of being, helping		
	Review: similes, metaphors		
	"k" (c, k, ck, qu) Words (anchor, chorus, circus, create, curious, kangaroo, kayak, napkin, nickel, pocket, quality, quiet, snack, squid); Dictionary		
Week 6	Story Writing, Independent Reading		
	Review: verbs-tense, phrases, agreement		
	Review: titles, dictionary guide words; thesaurus-synonyms, antonyms		
	Silent Letter (kn, gn, wr, wh) Words (answer, calf, design, gnaw, honor, hymn, knight, knife, listen, plumber, sword, thumb, wheeze, wrench); Dictionary		

		Skill Mastered	Needs Experience
Week 7	Grouping, Independent Reading		
	Review: adjectives, adverbs		
	Review: parts of a story		
	Double Consonant Words (suffer, shuffle, collar, valley, cattle, mitten, squirrel, mirror, riddle, giggle, pepper, rabbit, tunnel, essay); Dictionary		
Week 8	Memorization, Rhyming, Independent Reading		
	Review: homonyms, homophones, homographs		
	Friendly Letter (date, greeting, body, closing), envelope		
	Ordinal Number Words (eleventh, twelfth, thirteenth, fourteenth, fifteenth, sixteenth, seventeenth, eighteenth, nineteenth, twentieth, twenty-first, twenty-second, twenty-third, twenty-fourth, twenty-fifth); Dictionary		
Week 9	Observation, Story Writing, Independent Reading		
	4th Quarter Review		
	4th Quarter Review		
	4th Quarter Spelling Review		

Independent Reading List

Be sure to keep a record of the books your student is reading. There are spaces below for title, author, and the date of completion. It can be a positive experience for students as they see this list being filled in and know that they are mastering the important skill of reading. It can be helpful to know the authors and/or specific topics your student expresses interest in by allowing them to help make choices in selecting books. These selections should be fun for the student!

Book Title	Author	Date Completed

Book Title	Author	Date Completed

Language Level 4 – Independent Reading List

All books listed are published by Master Books or New Leaf Publishing Group.

Please select books that match your student's reading level. The books in each group are listed alphabetically, not according to the reading level.

Early Learner Board Books

A is for Adam

All God's Children

D is for Dinosaur

Inside Noah's Ark 4 Kids

It's Designed to Do What It Does Do

My Creation Bible

My Take-Along Bible

N is for Noah

Remarkable Rescue

Silver Ship — Great Creatures

When You See a Rainbow

When You See a Star

Early Learner Books Grades K-3

44 Animals of the Bible

Big Thoughts for Little Thinkers — Gospel

Big Thoughts for Little Thinkers — Missions

Big Thoughts for Little Thinkers — Scripture

Big Thoughts for Little Thinkers — Trinity

Charlie & Trike

Cool Creatures of the Ice Age

The Creation Story for Children

Dinosaurs: Stars of the Show

God is Really, Really Real

The Not So Super Skyscraper

Not Too Small at All

A Special Door

Tower of Babel

The True Account of Adam & Eve

The True Story of Noah's Ark

Whale of a Story

What Really Happened to the Dinosaurs?

When Dragon Hearts Were Good

Grades 4-6 Books

Answers Book for Kids, Vol. 1–8

The Complete Creation Museum Adventure

Dinosaurs by Design

Dinosaurs for Kids

Dinosaurs of Eden

Dry Bones and Other Fossils

God's Amazing Creatures and Me

How Many Animals Were on the Ark?

Inside Noah's Ark — Why it Worked

Life in the Great Ice Age

Marvels of Creation — Birds

Marvels of Creation — Mammals

Marvels of Creation — Sea Creatures

Men of Science, Men of God

Noah's Ark and the Ararat Adventure

Noah's Ark: Thinking Outside the Box

Operation Rawhide

The Story of In God We Trust

The Story of The Pledge of Allegiance

Why Is Keiko Sick?

Grades 7-8 Books

The 10-Minute Bible Study

The Building of the ARK Encounter

Champions of Invention

Champions of Mathematics

Champions of Science

Dragons of the Deep

Footprints in the Ash

The Great Alaskan Dinosaur Adventure

Great for God

If Animals Could Talk

Life Before Birth

Quick Answers to Tough Questions

Uncovering the Mysterious Woolly Mammoth

Create Your Own Dictionary!

The teacher may print off enough copies of the dictionary pages for each student to use for the course. A copy of all the dictionary pages may also be found on our website: www.masterbooks.com/classroom-aids.

The student may write the word and a simple definition for each entry. They may also choose to draw a small picture.

Language Level 4 – Create Your Own Dictionary!

Activities and Games

These games and activities are meant to add extra practice and fun to the lessons. They are optional, but most students will want to do as many as they can.

We encourage the student to create the cards used in the games. Writing out the words on the cards is part of the learning process.

The activities and games are in the order they are introduced in the course. Some games may have variations that cover concepts learned later in the course.

Supplies:

- Index cards
- Markers, crayons, stickers, etc.
- Three-hole punch and rings, or clips to store index cards (optional)

Matching Game

Focus:

- Days of the Week, Months of the Year, Weather, Homophones, Homonyms, Homographs, Memory, Syllables

Number of Players:

- One or more

Game Play:

- Have students write the days of the week on index cards — one day per card.

- Ask students what they do on Sunday. Have them draw it on a card. Continue with the remaining days until they have 14 cards — seven with the names of the week and seven with what they do each day.

- Turn the cards over and arrange them and play the memory game, matching the days with the student's drawings.

- When the game is over, have the student arrange the days of the week in order.

Bonus Challenge:

- Each time the student turns over a Day of the Week card, have them clap the syllables as they read it.

Game Variation:

- Repeat using the Months of the Year. Have students draw weather-related pictures for each month, including things they do.

- Have students write the names of the days of the week and/or months of the year on one set of notecards and their abbreviations on a second set. Mix them up and play the matching game.

- Have students write homophones, homonyms, and homographs, one per card. Have students draw a small picture on the card of what each word means. Mix them up and play the matching game.

I Spy Game

Focus:

- Nouns, Adjectives, Prepositions, Observation

Number of Players:

- Two or more

Game Play:

- The "spy" says, "I spy with my little eyes something . . ." then goes on to describe an object (noun) that is in the room.
- The other players try to guess what noun the person has spied by asking questions such as "Is it red?" or "Is it something you wear?"
- The game ends when the noun is discovered.

Game Variations:

- The spy must use adjectives to describe the object.
- Give each player a sheet of paper. Have the student create three columns by writing "person," "place," and "thing" across the top of the page. Each time a noun is discovered, have the students write the word under the correct column.
- Have the student write down the adjectives used. When the game is over, have them group the adjectives according to type, color, size, etc.
- Play the game normally, except have the spy use prepositions to describe the object. Example: "I spy with my little eyes something *over* the door." Players may also be required to name the preposition phrase, preposition, and/or the object of the preposition they used.

Simon Says

Focus:

- Nouns, Proper Nouns, Pronouns, Auditory Perception, Physical Activity

Number of Players:

- Two or more

Game Play:

- Each student should stand in front of a chair. "Simon" stands facing the student(s). Simon says a noun. If it is a proper noun, the student stays standing. If it is a common noun, the student sits. If the student sits when they should stand (or vice-versa), they are out. The last student standing wins. Pick a new Simon and play again!

Game Variations:

- When there are only two players, track how many nouns the player gets right in a row. Work to beat the highest record.

- Play the game using proper nouns and pronouns. The student should stand for the proper nouns and sit for the pronouns.

Charades

Focus:

- Action Verbs, Adverbs, Physical Activity

Number of Players:

- Two or more

Game Play:

- Have the student write a different action verb on at least ten index cards. Mix them up and put them in a pile, face down.

- Have the student draw a card and act out the verb.

- The teacher must guess the verb.

- Take turns being the actor until all the students and the teacher have had a turn and/ or all the cards are used.

Game Variations:

- Set a timer when the actor begins. Track how fast the player can guess the verb. Work to beat the quickest time.

- Divide players into teams. When it is their turn, the team picks a teammate to be the actor.

- Have students write down a different adverb on the same number of verb cards created for this game. Encourage students to pick adverbs that end in -ly as well as some that do not. Follow the game play rules, except the student must draw a verb card and an adverb card. The teacher must then guess the adverb and the verb.

Slap Jack!

Focus:

- Nouns, Possessive Nouns, Proper Nouns, Pronouns, Visual Processing

Number of Players:

- Two or more

Game Play:

- Ask students to write nouns on note cards. Students should write at least 20 regular nouns. Then they should write at least ten possessive nouns. Up to 52 cards may be created, with many more regular nouns than possessive nouns.

- Mix the cards up, then deal the cards clockwise, face down, until all the cards have been passed out. The players may not look at their cards.

- The player to the left of the dealer flips over one card, placing it in a pile in the middle of the table. This continues around the table, each person laying down a card on top of the pile in the middle of the table.

- The first player to slap their hand down on a possessive noun takes the possessive noun card and all the cards in the pile underneath it. They shuffle their new cards within the stack of cards they were dealt and place them face down in front of them.

- If a player slaps a noun that is not a possessive noun, they must give one card, face down, from their pile to the player who laid down the card.

- When the player has no more cards to turn over, they remain in the game until the next possessive noun is turned over. If they fail to win that pile, they are out of the game. The game continues until only one player has cards and wins the game.

Game Variations:

- When the player slaps a possessive noun card, they must use the possessive noun in a sentence to win the pile.

- Create at least ten cards with proper nouns or pronouns and replace the possessive noun cards. Players then watch for proper nouns (or pronouns) to slap.

Drawing Game

Focus:

- Subject, Predicate, Sentences, Creativity, Hand-Eye Coordination

Number of Players:

- Two or more

Game Play:

- Ask students to make two stacks of cards. Each stack should each have at least eight cards, equal in number. On the back side of the cards in one stack, write the word "Subject." Write "Predicate" on the back of the second stack.

- Ask the student to write sentences, except they will write the Subject part on one card and the Predicate part on the other.

- Shuffle the Subject stack, then shuffle the Predicate stack.

- The first player takes a card from each stack. The player must draw the sentence for the other players to guess.

Game Variations:

- Set a timer when the player begins to draw. Track how fast the player can guess the sentence. Work to beat the quickest time.

- Divide players into teams. When it is their turn, the team picks a teammate to draw the sentence.

Story Game

Focus:

- State of Being Verbs, Action Verbs, Helping Verbs, Linking Verbs, Memory, Creativity

Number of Players:

- Two or more

Game Play:

- Have the student write each state of being verb on index cards for a total of eight cards. Mix up the cards and lay the cards face down in a stack.

- The first player draws a card and starts off the story using the state of being verb on the card they drew. For example, if they drew the verb "are" they could say, "My family and neighbors are going to the zoo." (More than one sentence may be used if needed to set up the story and to use the verb correctly.)

- The next player draws a card and continues the story using the state of being verb they drew. The game ends when all the cards are used. The cards may be reshuffled and the game continued for as long as the game remains fun.

Bonus Challenge:

- Players can retell all the story parts before adding to the story.

Game Variations:

- Mix into the stack the Action Verb cards created for Charades.

- Write helping and/or linking verbs on cards and add them to the stack. When a player draws a card, have them identify what kind of verb it is.

Don't Make Me Laugh

Focus:

- Word Usage, Creativity

Number of Players:

- Two or more

Game Play:

- Ask students to make cards of the words they are learning to use such as a-an, see-saw-seen. Write all forms of each set of words on the card. If you use the list below, you should have 15 cards.

- Shuffle the cards and place them in a stack, face down. The first player draws a card. The player must say one or more sentences using all the words on the card correctly, with the intent of making the next player laugh. If the player fails to make the next player laugh, they must draw a new card and try again. Continue to play until all the cards are used. The stack may be reshuffled and the game continued as long as it remains fun.

Game Variations:

- Set a timer when the player draws the card. Track how fast the player takes to make the next player laugh. Work to beat the quickest time.

- Divide players into teams. When it is their turn, the team picks a teammate to be the player who tries to make the opposing team laugh.

- Add to the stack action, helping, linking, and state of being verbs, synonyms, antonyms, homophones, homonyms, and/or homographs.

Word List:

is, am, are	has, have, had	this, that, these, those
to, too, two	see, saw, seen	sit, set
there, their, they're	eat, ate, eaten	it's, its
a, an, the	go, went, gone	who's, whose
be, been, being	most, almost	real, really

Story Game

Focus:

- Synonyms, Antonyms, Homophones, Homonyms, Homographs, Auditory Perception, Memory, Creativity

Number of Players:

- Two or more

Game Play:

- Similar to the State of Being Verb Story Game, but with a twist. Students may either create a list of words to draw from or choose words as the game is played.

- The first player either draws a card or chooses a word. The next player must use a synonym of that word to start off the story.

- The player then draws a card or says a word for the next player. The next player then continues the story using a synonym of the word. The game continues until every player has had a turn or as long as the game is fun.

Bonus Challenge:

- Players can retell all the story parts before adding to the story.

Game Variations:

- Players must use the antonym of the word for their story.

- Players must use a homophone, homonym, and/or homograph in their story. This works best when cards are used. Have the student write sets of homophones, homonyms, and/or homographs on at least eight cards. The player whose turn it is to tell the next part of the story must use the homophone, homonym, or homograph twice, using the two different meanings. For example, if the homonym "him/hymn" is selected, the player might say, "I heard him sing a hymn."

Don't Make Me Laugh Version 2

Focus:

- Similes, Metaphors, Comparison, Creativity

Number of Players:

- Two or more

Game Play:

- Ask students to write nouns on note cards. Students should write at least 20 nouns.
- Create two piles of cards, face down.
- The first player draws one card from each pile.
- The player must use a simile to tell how the two nouns on the cards are alike using the word *as* or *like*. For example, if "dog" and "car" are the nouns, the player might say, "The dog is as fast as a car." The player should try to make the next player laugh. If the player fails to make the next player laugh, another set of cards is drawn and the player tries again. Continue to play until all the cards are used. The stacks may be shuffled, and the game continued as long as it remains fun.

Game Variations:

- Have the players compare the two nouns using words ending in *-er* or *-est*. Examples: "The dog is faster than the car." "The car is fast, but the dog is the fastest."
- Have players use a metaphor to compare the nouns.

Sandwich Game

Focus:

- Paragraphs, Memory, Creativity

Number of Players:

- Two or more

Game Play:

- Remind students that writing a paragraph is like making a sandwich. Use the sandwich image to guide students through the game.
- The player creates a topic sentence.
- The next player says the topic sentence, then adds the first detail sentence.
- The next player says the topic sentence, the first detail sentence, then adds a second detail sentence.
- The next player says the topic sentence, the first detail sentence, the second detail sentence, and adds a third detail sentence.
- The next player says the topic sentence, the first, second, and third detail sentences, then adds the concluding sentence.
- The next player recites the whole paragraph.
- The game can continue again for as long as it remains fun.

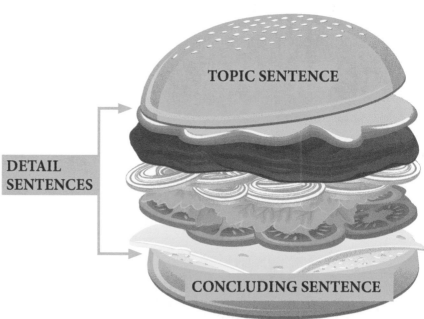

TOPIC SENTENCE

DETAIL SENTENCES

CONCLUDING SENTENCE

Story Game Version 2

Focus:

- Parts of a Story, Creativity

Number of Players:

- Two to seven

Game Play:

- Have the student create a sheet of paper or note card that lists the following:
  - Title
  - Characters
  - Setting
  - Plot-Beginning
  - Plot-Middle
  - Plot-End
  - Conclusion
- The first player chooses a title for the story.
- The second player chooses the characters for the story.
- The next player describes the setting of the story.
- The next player gives the beginning of the plot.
- The next player gives the middle of the plot.
- The next player gives the end of the plot.
- The last player gives the conclusion.
- If there are less than seven players, some players will repeat a turn and tell another part of the story.
- When the whole story is told, retell the story with each person retelling their part. The story should be told in a quick, cohesive manner this time around.
- The players may want to act out their play!

Sword Drills

Focus:

- Looking up Bible References, Memory

Number of Players:

- Two or more

Game Play:

- Players sit at a table with their Bible closed in front of them.
- The leader says, "Get your swords ready!"
- The leader gives a chapter and verse for the players to look up.
- The first player to find it stands up and reads the verse.
- Decide ahead of time how may Sword Drills will be done before the game ends. Five or ten are a good number.

Game Variations:

- Different groups may have different rules and ways of playing this game. If your student does Sword Drills at church or elsewhere, use those rules.
- Look up verses on a particular topic to use for the game such as faith, grace, or mercy. At the end of the game, see who can guess the theme chosen for the Sword Drills.

Spelling Practice

The research on how people learn to spell indicates that spelling mastery, in part, comes from spelling words correctly through the practice of writing. Words studied in isolation, in abstract lists, do not carry over from the study to correct use. To help a student learn how to spell a problem word, you can find the word's origins in a dictionary, study the prefixes and suffixes, and practice the basic spelling rules that apply. The spelling word lists on the next few pages can be used to help students know all the words from each lesson through the various spelling practice ideas provided. Then students may mark each word with a check mark to show their spelling word accomplishment.

Some students will need more practice than others when it comes to spelling. We have provided these ideas to help students who need the practice.

Magnetic Letters — Have students use the letters to put together their spelling words for the week.

Memory Game — Write half of the word on one index card and half of the word on the other. Play the Memory Game by having the student search for the other half of the word.

Memory Game — Write the word on one card and the definition on the other. Play the memory game.

Hot Potato — If you have several children, have them sit in a circle and toss around a small object like a bean bag. Play music. Shut the music off at random times (a small sand timer may also be used). Whoever has the "hot potato" when the music turns off must spell a word from their spelling list. (The teacher may choose the word for each student.) If the student spells the word correctly, they stay in the game.

Bingo — Play a game of bingo using spelling words for each square.

Spelling Bee — Hold a weekly spelling bee using the spelling words each student is working on.

One Letter at a Time — Have the student write the first letter of the word. Underneath that, have the student write the next two letters. Underneath the first two letters, have the student write the next three letters of the word. Continue until the entire word is written. Have the students write all the words for the week or just the ones they are having trouble with.

Charades — Play a game of charades using spelling words, except the players must spell the word they are guessing.

Flashcards — Have the student practice using the cards by looking at the word, turning the card over, and either spelling it to themselves, out loud, or by writing the word.

Right Brain Flashcards — Have the student write the word and draw pictures of the word or things that remind them how to spell it. Stickers and other items may be used. **Hint:** On the back side, the student can draw memory prompts. That side can be used to spell the word without looking at the word itself.

Word Board Games — Use board games that encourage spelling. Have students use their spelling words while playing them.

Internet Word Games — Search the Internet for safe, fun games that encourage spelling skills.

Word Shape Worksheets — Word shape worksheets for all of the spelling words are available as a free download at masterbooks.com/classroom-aids.

Spelling List

On the following pages are the spelling words from each lesson. You may choose to write out the words below that the student needs additional work on and to share this list with the student. Then you can work on those words together. **Note:** Students may want to put a star next to problem words each time they spell the word correctly in a sentence. Be sure to praise the student's progress as stars are accumulated.

(1) _____

(2) _____

(3) _____

(4) _____

(5) _____

(6) _____

(7) _____

(8) _____

(9) _____

(10) _____

(11) _____

(12) _____

(13) _____

(14) _____

(15) _____

(16) _____

(17) _____

(18) _____

(19) _____

(20) _____

(21) _____

(22) _____

(23) _____

(24) _____

(25) _____

(26) _____

(27) _____

(28) _____

(29) _____

(30) _____

(31) _____

(32) _____

(33) _____

(34) _____

(35) _____

(36) _____

(37) _____

(38) _____

(39) _____

(40) _____

(41) _____

(42) _____

(43) _____

(44) _____

(45) _____

(46) _____

(47) _____

(48) _____

(49) _____

(50) _____

Spelling Words

Lesson 1

- o break
- o drain
- o eight
- o flake
- o holiday
- o jail
- o past
- o shape
- o spam
- o stamp
- o steak
- o stray
- o talent
- o weigh

Lesson 2

- o alley
- o been
- o chief
- o desk
- o east
- o gently
- o green

- o leather
- o meant
- o niece
- o peach
- o speed
- o spent
- o squeeze

Lesson 3

- o align
- o build
- o deny
- o diet
- o flight
- o grind
- o height
- o inch
- o pilot
- o ruin
- o shine
- o sting
- o thigh
- o type

Lesson 4

- o broke
- o coast
- o crow
- o globe
- o goal
- o gold
- o growth
- o host
- o problem
- o shock
- o shop
- o shown
- o snow
- o wrote

Lesson 5

- o cute
- o done
- o fruit
- o glue
- o group
- o nephew
- o prove

- ○ punish
- ○ rescue
- ○ smooth
- ○ threw
- ○ truth
- ○ tube
- ○ unit

Lesson 6

- ○ crawl
- ○ drawn
- ○ exalt
- ○ false
- ○ faucet
- ○ fault
- ○ frown
- ○ howl
- ○ launch
- ○ mount
- ○ pounce
- ○ sauce
- ○ sound
- ○ sprout

Lesson 7

- ○ astound
- ○ bought
- ○ brought
- ○ caught
- ○ daughter
- ○ fought
- ○ found
- ○ fraught
- ○ ground
- ○ hound
- ○ ought
- ○ sought
- ○ taught
- ○ thought

Lesson 8

- ○ appear
- ○ board
- ○ career
- ○ course
- ○ dairy
- ○ declare
- ○ journey

- ○ learn
- ○ perhaps
- ○ purpose
- ○ score
- ○ sharp
- ○ twirl
- ○ worn

Lesson 9

- ○ _____
- ○ _____
- ○ _____
- ○ _____
- ○ _____
- ○ _____
- ○ _____
- ○ _____
- ○ _____
- ○ _____
- ○ _____
- ○ _____
- ○ _____

Lesson 10

- bedroom
- fingernail
- fireplace
- get-together
- homesick
- ice cream
- newspaper
- pinecone
- railroad
- seat belt
- sunflower
- tailgate
- twenty-one
- wheelchair

Lesson 11

- can't
- could've
- didn't
- don't
- haven't
- I'd
- I'm

- I've
- it's
- shouldn't
- wasn't
- won't
- would've
- you'd

Lesson 12

- boxes
- buses
- chimneys
- churches
- fleas
- foxes
- fusses
- heroes
- photos
- pianos
- rocks
- rodeos
- themes
- wishes

Lesson 13

- calves
- cliffs
- countries
- enemies
- halves
- ladies
- leaves
- lives
- mysteries
- roofs
- supplies
- twenties
- wives
- wolves

Lesson 14

- cacti
- children
- corn
- deer
- fish
- geese
- mice

- moose
- octopi
- oxen
- people
- seaweed
- sheep
- women

Lesson 15

- closer
- closest
- funnier
- funniest
- greater
- greatest
- hotter
- hottest
- larger
- largest
- redder
- reddest
- taller
- tallest

Lesson 16

- answer
- beggar
- calendar
- chapter
- collar
- director
- doctor
- labor
- motor
- polar
- proper
- sailor
- sugar
- weather

Lesson 17

- barrel
- battle
- candle
- eagle
- final
- metal
- model

- nickel
- pedal
- simple
- special
- title
- total
- towel

Lesson 18

- ○ _____
- ○ _____
- ○ _____
- ○ _____
- ○ _____
- ○ _____
- ○ _____
- ○ _____
- ○ _____
- ○ _____
- ○ _____
- ○ _____
- ○ _____
- ○ _____

Lesson 19

- bicycle
- decrease
- defeat
- misbehave
- misread
- nonsense
- octagon
- octopus
- overdone
- overheard
- quadrant
- triangle
- underground
- understand

Lesson 20

- actor
- builder
- colonial
- conductor
- creation
- dental
- enjoyment

- farmer
- illness
- kindness
- natural
- partial
- vacation
- wooden

Lesson 21

- disrupt
- erupt
- geography
- geology
- metric
- metronome
- odometer
- perimeter
- photocopy
- photograph
- subtract
- terrain
- territory
- traction

Lesson 22

- beat
- beet
- blew
- blue
- dear
- deer
- pain
- pane
- pray
- prey
- sail
- sale
- wait
- weight

Lesson 23

- bark
- bear
- change
- fire
- foot
- handle
- iron

- left
- organ
- pound
- rock
- rose
- squash
- trunk

Lesson 24

- bounce
- carrot
- citizen
- country
- cymbals
- damage
- edge
- gather
- ginger
- granted
- gymnastics
- include
- since
- yogurt

Lesson 25

- believe
- boiler
- brief
- ceiling
- cowboy
- destroy
- exploit
- receipt
- retrieve
- their
- toilet
- voyage
- weigh
- yield

Lesson 26

- alphabet
- afternoon
- behavior
- compromise
- direction
- document
- edible

- family
- following
- holiday
- internet
- navigate
- remember
- suddenly

Lesson 27

- _____
- _____
- _____
- _____
- _____
- _____
- _____
- _____
- _____
- _____
- _____
- _____
- _____

Lesson 28

- belong
- blanket
- bling
- drink
- frequent
- least
- saint
- scared
- scope
- skirt
- skunk
- starve
- swept
- tempt

Lesson 29

- attach
- brush
- challenge
- change
- chicken
- kitchen
- latch

- preach
- shape
- sharpen
- stretch
- thank
- thirsty
- watch

Lesson 30

- scramble
- scrape
- shrimp
- shrug
- split
- splurge
- sprain
- sprout
- square
- squat
- strain
- strip
- thread
- throat

Lesson 31

- awful
- elephant
- enough
- forever
- fossil
- freedom
- gopher
- graph
- laugh
- nephew
- phone
- phrase
- physical
- rough

Lesson 32

- anchor
- chorus
- circus
- create
- curious
- kangaroo
- kayak

- napkin
- nickel
- pocket
- quality
- quiet
- snack
- squid

Lesson 33

- answer
- calf
- design
- gnaw
- honor
- hymn
- knight
- knife
- listen
- plumber
- sword
- thumb
- wheeze
- wrench

Lesson 34

- cattle
- collar
- essay
- giggle
- mirror
- mitten
- pepper
- rabbit
- riddle
- shuffle
- squirrel
- suffer
- tunnel
- valley

Lesson 35

- eleventh
- twelfth
- thirteenth
- fourteenth
- fifteenth
- sixteenth
- seventeenth

- eighteenth
- nineteenth
- twentieth
- twenty-first
- twenty-second
- twenty-third
- twenty-fourth

Lesson 36

- _____
- _____
- _____
- _____
- _____
- _____
- _____
- _____
- _____
- _____
- _____
- _____
- _____

Sight Words

We have provided sight words from previous levels. Please be sure the student can read these words easily. If not, practice them regularly until they are mastered.

Sight words the student has mastered in *Foundations Phonics*:

- a
- all
- an
- and
- are
- as
- at
- be
- belong
- but
- by
- can
- did
- for
- from
- get
- had
- has

- have
- he
- his
- how
- I
- if
- in
- is
- it
- my
- no
- not
- of
- on
- or
- out
- see
- she

- so
- than
- that
- the
- them
- then
- they
- this
- to
- was
- we
- what
- when
- who
- will
- you
- your

Sight words the student has mastered in *Language Lessons for a Living Education Level 2*:

o always	o gave	o these
o around	o goes	o those
o because	o green	o upon
o been	o its	o us
o before	o made	o use
o best	o many	o very
o both	o off	o wash
o buy	o or	o which
o call	o pull	o why
o cold	o read	o wish
o does	o right	o work
o don't	o sing	o would
o fast	o sit	o write
o first	o sleep	o your
o five	o tell	
o found	o their	

Sight words the student has mastered in *Language Lessons for a Living Education Level 3*:

○ about
○ better
○ bring
○ carry
○ clean
○ cut
○ done
○ draw
○ drink
○ eight
○ fall
○ far
○ full
○ got

○ grow
○ hold
○ hot
○ hurt
○ if
○ keep
○ laugh
○ light
○ long
○ much
○ myself
○ never
○ only
○ own

○ pick
○ seven
○ shall
○ show
○ six
○ small
○ start
○ ten
○ today
○ together
○ try
○ warm

Sight words the student has mastered in *Language Lessons for a Living Education Level 4*:

○ apple	○ girl	○ rabbit
○ bear	○ goodbye	○ robin
○ birthday	○ ground	○ school
○ bread	○ horse	○ shoe
○ brother	○ house	○ sister
○ chair	○ kitty	○ squirrel
○ chicken	○ letter	○ street
○ children	○ money	○ table
○ Christmas	○ morning	○ thing
○ door	○ mother	○ watch
○ farmer	○ night	○ water
○ father	○ paper	○ window
○ flower	○ party	
○ garden	○ picture	

Books of the Bible

Genesis	Isaiah	Romans
Exodus	Jeremiah	1st Corinthians
Leviticus	Lamentations	2nd Corinthians
Numbers	Ezekiel	Galatians
Deuteronomy	Daniel	Ephesians
Joshua	Hosea	Philippians
Judges	Joel	Colossians
Ruth	Amos	1st Thessalonians
1st Samuel	Obadiah	2nd Thessalonians
2nd Samuel	Jonah	1st Timothy
1st Kings	Micah	2nd Timothy
2nd Kings	Nahum	Titus
1st Chronicles	Habakkuk	Philemon
2nd Chronicles	Zephaniah	Hebrews
Ezra	Haggai	James
Nehemiah	Zechariah	1st Peter
Esther	Malachi	2nd Peter
Job	Matthew	1st John
Psalms	Mark	2nd John
Proverbs	Luke	3rd John
Ecclesiastes	John	Jude
Song of Solomon	Acts	Revelation

Genres of the Bible

Teacher Note: There are many ways to classify the genres of Scripture. We have used the classification found on the Answers in Genesis website.

Law	Major Prophets	History
Genesis	Isaiah	Acts
Exodus	Jeremiah	**Letter**
Leviticus	Lamentations	Romans
Numbers	Ezekiel	Ist Corinthians
Deuteronomy	Daniel	2nd Corinthians
History	**Minor Prophets**	Galatians
Joshua	Hosea	Ephesians
Judges	Joel	Philippians
Ruth	Amos	Colossians
Ist Samuel	Obadiah	Ist Thessalonians
2nd Samuel	Jonah	2nd Thessalonians
Ist Kings	Micah	Ist Timothy
2nd Kings	Nahum	2nd Timothy
Ist Chronicles	Habakkuk	Titus
2nd Chronicles	Zephaniah	Philemon
Ezra	Haggai	Hebrews
Nehemiah	Zechariah	James
Esther	Malachi	Ist Peter
Poetry	**Gospel**	2nd Peter
Job	Matthew	Ist John
Psalms	Mark	2nd John
Proverbs	Luke	3rd John
Ecclesiastes	John	Jude
Song of Solomon		Revelation

Genres are based on *Books of the Bible Flashcards* from Answers in Genesis.

Copywork Practice

(1) A noun is a person, place, or thing.

_____

_____

(2) A proper noun names a noun and begins with a capital letter.

_____

_____

(3) Singular means one.

_____

(4) Plural means more than one.

_____

(5) A pronoun stands for another noun.

_____

_____

(6) An adjective is a word that describes a person, place, or thing.

_____

_____

(7) An adverb tells about a verb.

_____

_____

(8) A possessive noun shows who or what owns or has something.

_____

_____

(9) A quotation is when you copy exactly what someone has said.

_____

_____

(10) An action verb tells what is happening in a sentence.

_____

_____

(11) Some verbs show a state of being rather than action.

_____

_____

(12) A preposition is a word that links a noun (or pronoun) to another word in the sentence.

_____

_____

_____

(13) When we write a paragraph, we start with a topic sentence.

_____

_____

We add two or three detail sentences.

_____

_____

We end with a concluding sentence.

_____

_____

(14) Compound words are two words made into one, which gives it a new meaning.

_____

_____

_____

(15) Synonyms are two words that mean the same thing.

_____

_____

(16) Antonyms are two words that have opposite meanings.

_____

_____

(17) Homonyms are words that sound the same, mean something different, and are spelled the same.

_____

_____

_____

(18) Homophones are words that sound the same, mean something different, and are spelled differently.

_____

_____

_____

(19) Homographs are two words that do not sound the same, have different meanings, and are spelled the same.

_____

_____

_____

(20) Truth means something that is true or real.

_____

_____

(21) Fiction is a story that is made up or not true.

_____

_____

(22) A fact is something that can be proven to be true or false.

_____

_____

(23) An opinion is a feeling, belief, or an attitude. It cannot be proven to be true or false.

_____

_____

_____

(24) A figure of speech describes something in a way that is not literal. The meaning is not exactly what is written.

_____

_____

_____

(25) A simile compares two different things using the words like or as.

_____

_____

(26) A metaphor compares two different things without using the words like or as.

_____

_____

_____

(27) The subject tells who or what the sentence is about.

_____

_____

(28) The predicate tells what the subject does or is.

_____

_____

(29) A contraction is two words that are shortened into one, with an apostrophe in place of the letter that was removed.

_____

_____

_____

_____

(30) A root word is a word to which we add a prefix or suffix.

_____

_____

(31) Initials are the first letters of the first, middle, or last name of a person, followed by a period.

_____

_____

_____

(32) An abbreviation is the shortened form of a word.

_____

_____

(33) Mister is the title of a man.

_____

_____

(34) Miss is the title of an unmarried woman.

_____

_____

(35) Missus is the title of a married woman.

_____

_____

Days of the Week Practice

Sunday = Sun.

_____

Monday = Mon.

_____

Tuesday = Tues.

_____

Wednesday = Wed.

_____

Thursday = Thurs.

_____

Friday = Fri.

_____

Saturday = Sat.

_____

Months of the Year Practice

January = Jan.

_____

February = Feb.

_____

March = Mar.

_____

April = Apr.

_____

May = May

_____

June = June

_____

July = July

_____

August = Aug.

_____

September = Sept.

_____

October = Oct.

_____

November = Nov.

_____

December = Dec.

_____

Days of the Month Poem Practice

Days of the Month Poem

    30 days has September,
    April, June, and November
    All the rest have 31
    Except for February
    Which has 28
    But 29 in a leap year

_____

_____

_____

_____

_____

_____

Ordinal Number Practice

(1) first _____

(2) second _____

(3) third _____

(4) fourth _____

(5) fifth _____

(6) sixth _____

(7) seventh _____

(8) eighth _____

(9) ninth _____

(10) tenth _____

(11) eleventh _____

(12) twelfth _____

(13) thirteenth _____

(14) fourteenth _____

(15) fifteenth _____

(16) sixteenth _____

(17) seventeenth _____

(18) eighteenth _____

(19) nineteenth _____

(20) twentieth _____

(21) twenty-first _____

(22) twenty-second _____

(23) twenty-third _____

(24) twenty-fourth _____

(25) twenty-fifth _____

Contraction Practice

(1) here is _____

(2) do not _____

(3) can not _____

(4) he is _____

(5) we would _____

(6) I am _____

(7) she will _____

(8) they are _____

(9) are not _____

(10) does not _____

(11) he would _____

(12) I have _____

(13) must not _____

(14) she has _____

(15) there is _____

(16) will not _____

(17) did not _____

(18) it is _____

(19) it has _____

(20) she would _____

(21) they have _____

(22) was not _____

(23) we are _____

(24) who will _____

(25) you are _____

(26) could have _____

(27) have not _____

(28) I would _____

(29) should not _____

(30) would have _____

(31) you would _____

Titles Practice

Write the abbreviation for each title.

Mister _____   Professor _____

Miss _____   Honorable _____

Missus _____   Senator _____

Doctor _____   President _____

Reverend _____   Captain _____

Detective _____   General _____

Sergeant _____   Junior _____

Representative _____   Senior _____

States and State Abbreviation Practice

Copy name, postal code, and abbreviation for each state.

(1) Alabama   AL   Ala.

_____

(2) Alaska   AK

_____

(3) Arizona   AZ   Ariz.

_____

(4) Arkansas   AR   Ark.

_____

(5) California   CA   Calif.

_____

(6) Colorado   CO   Colo.

_____

(7) Connecticut   CT   Conn.

_____

(8) Delaware   DE   Del.

---

(9) Florida   FL   Fla.

---

(10) Georgia   GA   Ga.

---

(11) Hawaii   HI

---

(12) Idaho   ID

---

(13) Illinois   IL   Ill.

---

(14) Indiana   IN   Ind.

---

(15) Iowa   IA

---

(16) Kansas	KS	Kan.
(17) Kentucky	KY	Ky.
(18) Louisiana	LA	La.
(19) Maine	ME	Me.
(20) Maryland	MD	Md.
(21) Massachusetts	MA	Mass.
(22) Michigan	MI	Mich.
(23) Minnesota	MN	Minn.

(24) Mississippi	MS	Miss.
(25) Missouri	MO	Mo.
(26) Montana	MT	Mont.
(27) Nebraska	NE	Neb.
(28) Nevada	NV	Nev.
(29) New Hampshire	NH	N.H.
(30) New Jersey	NJ	N.J.
(31) New Mexico	NM	N.M.

(32)	New York	NY	N.Y.
(33)	North Carolina	NC	N.C.
(34)	North Dakota	ND	N.D.
(35)	Ohio	OH	
(36)	Oklahoma	OK	Okla.
(37)	Oregon	OR	Or.
(38)	Pennsylvania	PA	Pa.
(39)	Rhode Island	RI	R.I.

(40) South Carolina	SC	S.C.	
(41) South Dakota	SD	S.D.	
(42) Tennessee	TN	Tenn.	
(43) Texas	TX	Tex.	
(44) Utah	UT		
(45) Vermont	VT	Vt.	
(46) Virginia	VA	Va.	
(47) Washington	WA	Wash.	

(48) West Virginia   WV   W. Va.

_____

(49) Wisconsin   WI   Wis.

_____

(50) Wyoming   WY   Wyo.

_____

Calendar Study Sheets

There are 7 days in a week:

Sunday, Monday, Tuesday, Wednesday, Thursday, Friday, Saturday

There are 12 months in a year:

January, February, March, April, May, June, July, August, September, October, November, December

There are 24 hours in a day.

There are 365 days in a year.

Seasons of the Year

Spring = March, April, May (warm)

Summer = June, July, August (hot)

Fall = September, October, November (cool)

Winter = December, January, February (cold)

Here is how you write a date:

January 1, 2022

Grammar Study Sheets

Types of Sentences

Imperative:	gives a command; ends with a period
Declarative:	makes a statement; ends with a period
Exclamatory:	expresses strong emotion; ends with an exclamation point
Interrogative:	asks a question; ends with a question mark

Noun

A noun is a person, place, or thing.

Proper Noun

A proper noun names a noun and begins with a capital letter.

Possessive Noun

A possessive noun shows who or what owns or has something. We make a singular noun possessive by adding an apostrophe and an -s. We make a plural noun that ends in an -s possessive by adding the apostrophe to the end of the word.

Pronoun

A pronoun stands for another noun. When a pronoun takes the place of more than one noun, it is called a plural pronoun.

Singular Pronouns	Plural Pronouns
I, you, it	us
she, her	we
he, him	them

We do not add an *apostrophe* or an *apostrophe s* to pronouns to make them possessive.

Possessive Pronouns
my, your, his, her, its, our, their

Pronouns that can Stand Alone
mine, yours, ours, his, hers, theirs

Note: The pronoun *his* can be used with a regular possessive pronoun, and it can stand alone.

Plural Noun

Plural nouns name more than one person, place, or thing.

plural = add -s
ends in s, ss, sh, ch, z, or x = add -es

vowel + y, add -s	vowel + o, add -s	consonant + o, add -es

piano = pianos	photo = photos

Ends in f or fe = change f or fe
to v and add -es

roof = roofs	cliff = cliffs

When a word ends in a consonant and the letter y, we make it plural by changing the y to i and then add -es.

Single	Plural	Single	Plural
man	men	goose	geese
woman	women	mouse	mice
child	children	ox	oxen
person	people	octopus	octopi
		cactus	cacti

Single	Plural	Single	Plural
deer	deer	moose	moose
fish	fish	corn	corn
sheep	sheep	seaweed	seaweed

Antecedent

The antecedent is the noun or nouns the pronoun stands for.

Adjective

An adjective is a word that describes a person, place, or thing.

Adjectives describe: colors, sizes, shapes,
tastes, smells, sounds,
looks, feels, how many,
weather, feelings, behaviors

Adverb

Adverbs tell about a verb. An adverb often ends in -ly and describes how, when, where, or how often a verb happens.

There are many adverbs. Here is a list of examples to study:

How	When	Where	How Often
gently	early	above	daily
quickly	now	inside	never
quietly	soon	here	often
sadly	tomorrow	outside	usually
safely	yesterday	upstairs	yearly

Articles

Articles come before a noun and are a type of adjective.
Use *a* before words that start with a consonant.
Use *an* before words that start with a vowel.
Use *the* to refer to a specific noun.

Quotation

A quotation is when you copy exactly what someone has said.

- Remember to use a comma before the quote.
- Remember to use a capital letter to start the first word of the quote.
- Remember to use quotation marks before and after the quote.

Preposition

A preposition is a word that links a noun (or pronoun) to another word in the sentence. It shows a relationship between a noun and another word.

A prepositional phrase begins with a preposition and ends with a noun.

The noun (or pronoun) the preposition refers to is called the *object of the preposition.*

Prepositions show location. These are common prepositions:

above	on	inside	in
below	off	outside	to
over	before	with	into
under	after	through	by
behind	beside	between	near

Some prepositions can refer to time:

at	of	until	from
on	to	after	upon
in	since	before	past
by	during	through	about

Sentences

A sentence must end in a punctuation mark:

period .	question mark ?	exclamation point !

Subject — Predicate

Subject tells who or what the sentence is about.

Predicate tells what the subject does or is.

A compound subject has more than one subject.

A compound predicate has more than one predicate.

Compound Words

Compound words are two words made into one with a new meaning.

Commas

We use a comma when we write a list of things in a sentence.

We use a comma when we address someone.
- o When the person's name is first in a sentence, the comma goes after the name.
- o When the name comes in the middle of the sentence, a comma goes before and after the name.
- o When the name comes at the end of the sentence, a comma goes before the name.

Conjunctions

Conjunctions are words that join two words or phrases together. We can combine sentences by using a conjunction.

for   and   nor   but   or   yet   so

The first letter of each conjunction spells fanboys.

Interjections

Interjections are words that express emotion or feelings. Often, they are found at the beginning of a sentence and are followed by an exclamation point.

Action Verbs

Action verbs tell what is happening in a sentence.

State of Being Verbs

State of being verbs show state of being rather than action. They link the subject to the predicate.

The Eight State of Being Verbs:

is	are	were	been
am	was	be	being

Linking Verbs

Linking verbs link a noun or adjective to the subject of the sentence. When a state of being verb is not acting like a helping verb, it is a linking verb.

Helping Verbs

Helping verbs help another verb in a sentence. They come before the main verb.

has have had	do does did
can will shall	could would should
must may might	

Verb Phrases

A phrase is a small group of words. A verb phrase is a helping verb (or helping verb phrase) and the main verb. A helping verb phrase is a small group of helping verbs.

can be has been	could be have been	may be had been	might be might have been

Verb Tense

A verb can tell us whether the sentence takes place in the past, present, or future.

I ran fast. (Past)
I run fast. (Present)
I will run fast. (Future)

Verb Agreement

When we write a sentence, the subject and the linking verb must agree. We need to use the correct linking verb with our subject.
- First, we look at our subject. Is it singular or plural?
- Then we look at our linking verb. Is it present or past tense?

Subject	Present Tense	Past Tense
Singular: he, she, it	is	was
Plural: we, they, you	are	were
I	am	was

Paragraph

A paragraph is a group of sentences about a specific idea or topic. A paragraph should:

- Start on a new line with an indent.
- Include at least four sentences.
- Start with a topic sentence.
- Include 2-3 sentences that give details about the topic.
- End with a concluding sentence. This sentence ends the paragraph by saying the topic in another way.

The Eight Parts of Speech:

Noun = person, place, thing
Example: cat, yard, ball

Verb = shows action or state of being.
Examples: ran, jump, is, am

Adjective = describes a noun or pronoun. It tells what kind, how many, which one.
Examples: red, five, bumpy

Adverb = describes a verb, adjective, or another adverb. It tells when, where, how, or how often.
Examples: after, inside, gently, always

Pronoun = takes the place of a noun.
Examples: he, she, it

Conjunction = joins words or phrases.
Examples: and, or, but

Preposition = describes a relationship between a noun or pronoun and another word that follows it.
Examples: to, for, with

Interjection = expresses strong feeling or emotion. Often followed by an exclamation point.
Examples: Hi! Ouch! Yes!

Acronym

An acronym uses the first letters of a group of words to form a new word. The acronym stands for the original group of words. Example: Fanboys is an acronym to help us remember a list of common conjunctions.

Homophones — Homonyms — Homographs

Homophones are words that sound the same, mean something different, and are spelled differently.

Homonyms are words that sound the same, mean something different, and are spelled the same.

Homographs are two words that do not sound the same, have different meanings, and are spelled the same.

Homophones:	Homonyms:	Homographs
· Sound the same	· Sound the same	· Sound different
· Different meanings	· Different meanings	· Different meanings
· Spelled differently	· Spelled the same	· Spelled the same

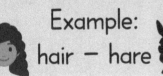

Example:
hair — hare

Example:
pen — pen

Example:
bass — bass

Synonyms – Antonyms

Synonyms are two words that mean the same thing.

Antonyms are two words that have opposite meanings.

Be – Been – Being

The verb *be* refers to the present.	The verb *been* refers to the past.	The verb *being* refers to the present and needs a helping verb.
I will be back soon.	I have been gone a while.	I am being chased by a dog.

Eat – Ate – Eaten

The verb *eat* refers to the present.	The verb *ate* refers to the past.	The verb *eaten* refers to the past and needs a helping verb.
I eat.	I ate.	I have eaten.

Go – Went – Gone

The verb *go* refers to the present.	The verb *went* refers to the past.	The verb *gone* refers to the past. It needs a helping verb.
I go.	I went.	I have gone.

Has – Have – Had

The helping verbs *has* and *have* are in the present and show there is possession.

have		has	
I have	they have	he has	she has
you have	we have	it has	

When we are talking about something in the past, we use the word *had*.

Is – Am – Are

is = one, present tense
am = one, present tense
are = more than one, present tense

It's — Its

it's = it is	(!)	its = possession (and breaks the rules)
It's going to be a great day.		Give the dog its bone.

Most — Almost

most = the largest amount	almost = nearly

Real — Really

real = it exists. It is not pretend or made up.	really = very

See — Saw — Seen

The verb *see* refers to the present.	The verb *saw* refers to the past.	The verb *seen* refers to the past and needs a helping verb.
I see.	I saw.	I have seen.

Sit – Set

sit = rest in an upright position	set = place an object
I like to sit in my new chair.	I set my lunch on the table.

There – Their – They're

there = a place
their = belonging to others
they're = a contraction that means "they are"

This – That – These – Those

	Near	Far
Singular	this	that
Plural	these	those

To – Too – Two

to = direction	too = also or a lot	two = number

Whose – Who's

who's = who is		whose = possession (and breaks the rules)

Root Word

Root words are the words we add a suffix or a prefix to.

$$rupt = break\ or\ burst$$
$$terr = land$$
$$geo = earth,\ ground,\ or\ soil$$
$$photo = light$$
$$tract = pull\ or\ drag$$
$$meter\ or\ metr = measure$$

Prefix

A prefix is letters added to the beginning of a word to change the meaning.

un- = not

re- = again

in- = not, in, or on

im- = not, in, or on (use im- for words that begin with b, m, and p)

dis- = not or opposite of

pre- = before

tele- = far or distant

bi- = two

non- = not

oct- = eight

quad- = four

under- = too little, below

mis- = bad or wrong

over- = too much, above

tri- = three

de- = reduce, remove, get off from, or do the opposite of

Suffix

A suffix is letters added to the end of a word to change the meaning.

-s, -es = plural, more than one
-ed = past tense
-ful = full of
-ing = action, process
-est = superlative (utmost) degree
-les = without
-al = related to, character of
-er = one who, that which
-ness = condition, state of
-or = one who, that which
-en = become, made of, resemble, to make
-ial = related to, character of
-ment = act, process
-tion = act, result, or state of

Suffix -ed, -ing

Root word ends with a silent e	= drop the e before adding the suffix
Root word has one syllable, one short vowel, and ends with one consonant	= double the consonant then add -ed or -ing.

kick : kicked, kicking
bake : baked, baking
stop : stopped, stopping

Suffix -er, -est

When the word ends in the letter e, drop the final e before adding -er or -est.

When the word ends in the letter y, change the y to an i before adding -er or -est.

When the word contains a short vowel, double the final consonant before adding -er or -est.

Truth/Fiction

Truth means something that is true or real.

Fiction is a story that is made up or not true.

Fact/Opinion

A fact is something that can be proven to be true or false.

An opinion is a feeling, belief, or an attitude. It cannot be proven to be true or false.

Figure of Speech

A figure of speech describes something in a way that is not literal. The meaning is not exactly what is written. It is figurative.

Simile

A simile is a figure of speech. It compares two different things using the words *like* or *as*.

Metaphor

A metaphor is also a figure of speech. It compares two different things without using the words *like* or *as*.

Contractions

Contractions are two words that are shortened into one, with an apostrophe in place of the missing letters.

Common Contractions

could've = could have
haven't = have not
doesn't = does not
shouldn't = should not
would've = would have
they've = they have
mustn't = must not
there's = there is
you'd = you would
I'd = I would
he's = he is
here's = here is

she'll = she will
we'd = we would
aren't = are not
he'd = he would
I've = I have
she's = she is
it's = it is
she'd = she would
wasn't = was not
we're = we are
who'll = who will

Initials

Initials are the first letter of the first, middle, or last name of a person.

Titles

Mister is the title of a man.
Miss is the title of an unmarried woman.
Missus is the title of a married woman.

We can abbreviate these titles.

Mister = Mr.
Miss = Ms.
Missus = Mrs.
Junior = Jr.
Senior = Sr.

We can abbreviate other titles.

Doctor = Dr.
Reverend = Rev.
Detective = Det.
Professor = Prof.

We can abbreviate titles related
to our government.

Honorable = Hon.
Senator = Sen.
Representative = Rep.
President = Pres.

We can abbreviate titles related
to our military.

Captain = Capt.
General = Gen.
Sergeant = Sgt.

We can abbreviate streets.

Avenue = Ave.
Drive = Dr.
Land = Ln.
Road = Rd.
Route = Rt.
Street = St.
Boulevard = Blvd.

Court = Ct.
Highway = Hwy.
Parkway = Pkwy.
Place = Pl.
Terrace = Terr.
Turnpike = Tpke.

Titles of Books, Magazines, Movies, and Plays

When you write a sentence using the title of a book, magazine, movie, or play, you should:
- o Underline the title (or use italics if you are using a computer)
- o Capitalize the first and last word
- o Capitalize all other words except small words that are not nouns, verbs, or adjectives such as: *the, for, and*

Parts of a Story

The *title* is the name of a book.

The *author* is who wrote the book.

Characters are the people or animals in the story.

The *setting* is where and when a story takes place. The setting can be a small place like a kitchen or a big place like a town. A story can take place long ago or just yesterday.

The *plot* is what happens in the story. It tells us what the conflict or the problem is, what happens, and how the conflict or problem is solved. It has a beginning, middle, and end.

The *conclusion*, or ending, answers any questions that need to be answered and wraps up the story.

Writing a Letter

When you write a letter, make sure to put the parts of your letter in the correct place:

o date

o greeting

o body

o closing

o signature

Addressing an Envelope

When you address an envelope, be sure to put each address in the correct place. An address includes:

o First and Last Name

o House Number and Street Name

o City, State Abbreviation, and Zip Code

Answers for the numbered problems are provided here
with the exception of the Narration Practice questions.

Language Lessons for a Living Education Level 4 ⟶ Worksheet Answer Keys

Answers are given for numbered problems on the worksheets.

Lesson 1; Exercise 1; Day 1

1. Possible answer: yellow : sun : : green : grass
2. Possible answer: kitten : cat : : puppy : dog

Lesson 1; Exercise 3; Day 3

1. Imperative — gives a command
2. Declarative — makes a statement
3. Exclamatory — expresses strong emotion
4. Interrogative — asks a question
5. Imperative .
6. Declarative .
7. Exclamatory !
8. Interrogative ?

Lesson 1; Exercise 5; Day 5

1. past, stamp
2. spam, talent
3. holiday, stray
4. drain, jail
5. flake, shape
6. break, steak
7. eight, weigh

Lesson 2; Exercise 2; Day 7

1. car's
2. dog's
3. cats'
4. bowls'

Lesson 2; Exercise 3; Day 8

1. Micah was nervous about his new class?
2. Dad said Micah would learn a life lesson.
3. Alexia wanted
4. micah might make some new friends.
5. He had a lot on his mind!

6. Micah wanted Jin in his class.
7. Micah was the youngest in his class.
8. Micah jumped into the car.
9. Alexia smiled at him.

Lesson 2; Exercise 5; Day 10

1. alley, gently
2. meant, leather
3. been
4. peach, east
5. speed, green
6. chief, niece
7. desk, spent
8. squeeze

Lesson 3; Exercise 1; Day 11

1. Both
2. Map B
3. Map B
4. Map A
5. Both

Lesson 3; Exercise 2; Day 12

1. I
2. We
3. Claire and I
4.

Lesson 3; Exercise 3; Day 13

1. fanboys
2. for

   and

   nor

   but

   or

   yet

   so
3. 4 and 9

Lesson 3; Exercise 5; Day 15

1. inch, sting
2. ruin, build
3. shine
4. type, height, diet, align
5. deny
6. grind, pilot
7. flight, thigh

Lesson 4; Exercise 1; Day 16

Lesson 4; Exercise 2; Day 17

1. my
2. class

Lesson 4; Exercise 3; Day 18

1. An owl and bat
2. and
3. and
4. sat and hatched the three eggs.
5.

Lesson 4; Exercise 5; Day 20

1. problem, shop, shock
2. coast, goal
3. broke, wrote, globe
4. crow, snow, growth, shown
5. gold, host

Lesson 5; Exercise 1; Day 21

1. 3, 4, 1, 2

Lesson 5; Exercise 2; Day 22

1. blew

Lesson 5; Exercise 3; Day 23

1. Micah said, "Jin, come see the Temple in my class."
2. "It took a long time to build this Temple," said Mr. C.

Lesson 5; Exercise 5; Day 25

1. punish
2. done
3. nephew
4. rescue
5. cute
6. unit
7. smooth

8. group

9. truth

10. glue

11. tube

12. threw

13. fruit

14. prove

Lesson 6; Exercise 2; Day 27

1. The children should wash their hands.

2. The family will eat supper soon.

3. They must pray before they eat.

4. They might eat pie for dessert.

5. Dad shall wash the dishes.

Lesson 6; Exercise 3; Day 28

1. Does Claire know about the Temple, Micah?

2. Claire, did you see the Temple?

3. How long, Mr. Cunningham, did it take to build?

Lesson 6; Exercise 5; Day 30

1. false, exalt

2. fault, faucet, launch

3. drawn, crawl

4. sauce

5. pounce

6. frown, howl

7. mount, sprout, sound

Lesson 7; Exercise 2; Day 32

1. is or was

2. has or had

3. did, does, can, will, shall, could, would, should, must, may, or might

4. are or were

5. Micah does play with building blocks.

6. Jin will help Micah.

7. Micah and Jin should clean the room first.

8. The boys might build a tent with their building blocks.

9. The boys were building the tower quickly.

10. Sentence 9

Lesson 7; Exercise 3; Day 33

1. Dinosaurs by Design has a lot of good information.

2. I was in a play called The Christmas Story.

3. Have you watched A Jurassic Ark Mystery by Buddy Davis?

4. Swamp Man!

5. Life in the Great Ice Age

6. The Flood of Noah

7. I Dig Dinosaurs

Lesson 7; Exercise 5; Day 35

1. caught, fraught, daughter, taught

2. ought, brought, sought, fought, thought, bought

3. found, hound, ground, astound

Lesson 8; Exercise 2; Day 37

1. H

2. L

3. H

4. L

Lesson 8; Exercise 3; Day 38

1. mad

2. confused

3. happy

4. laughing

5. sad

6. sleepy

Lesson 8; Exercise 5; Day 40

1. sharp

2. dairy, declare

3. twirl, perhaps, purpose

4. learn, journey

5. appear, career

6. worn, board, score, course

Lesson 9; Exercise 2; Day 42

1. Answers will vary. A capital letter should start each word of the state's name.

2. Answers will vary. A capital letter should start each word of the city's name.

3. boy's

4. cat's

5. I

6. We

7. Claire and I

8. my

9. class

10. An owl and bat

11. and

12. Answers will vary.

13. Micah does play with building blocks.

14. Jin will help Micah.

15. Micah and Jin should clean the room first.

16. The boys might build a tent with their building blocks.

17. The boys were building the tower quickly.

18. were

19. H

20. L

21.

Lesson 9; Exercise 3; Day 43

1. Imperative — asks a question
2. Declarative — expresses strong emotion
3. Exclamatory — makes a statement
4. Interrogative — gives a command

5. Micah jumped into the car.

6. Alexia smiled at him.

7. Micah went for a walk with Jin and Claire.

8. Answers may vary. Check for correct use of an interjection, capitalization, and punctuation.

9. F = for

10. A = and

11. N = nor

12. B = but

13. O = or

14. Y = yet

15. S = so

16. Claire asked, "Did you show Jin the Temple?"

17. Does Claire know about the Temple, Micah?

18. Claire, did you see the Temple?

19. How long, Mr. Cunningham, did it take to build?

20. Dinosaurs by Design has a lot of good information.

21. I was in a play called The Christmas Story.

22. Have you watched A Jurassic Ark Mystery by Buddy Davis?

23. Swamp Man!

24. Life in the Great Ice Age

25. Answers will vary.

Lesson 10; Exercise 1; Day 46

1. sunny
2. bikes
3. 4
4. 11
5. 27

Lesson 10; Exercise 2; Day 47

1. future
2. past
3. present
4. call
5. live
6. eat

Lesson 10; Exercise 3; Day 48

1. hope
2. hornet
3. hoot
4. huge
5. house
6. howl
7. chēp
8. skāl
9. nāl
10. brōk

11. D

Lesson 10; Exercise 5; Day 50

1. homesick
2. fingernail
3. bedroom
4. tailgate
5. pinecone
6. sunflower
7. fireplace
8. railroad
9. wheelchair
10. newspaper
11. twenty-one
12. get-together
13. seat belt
14. ice cream

Lesson 11; Exercise 2; Day 52

1. could be
2. could be eating

Lesson 11; Exercise 3; Day 53

1. can't — can not
2. don't — do not
3. he's — he is
4. here's — here is

5. I'm — I am
6. she'll — she will
7. they're — they are
8. we'd — we would

9. are not = aren't
10. does not = doesn't
11. he would = he'd
12. I have = I've
13. must not = mustn't
14. she has = she's
15. there is = there's

16. will not = won't
17. didn't = did not
18. it's = it is or it has
19. she'd = she would
20. they've = they have
21. wasn't = was not
22. we're = we are
23. who'll = who will
24. you're = you are

Lesson 11; Exercise 5; Day 55

1. It's about four hours before I leave on my trip.
2. I could've packed earlier, but I didn't have time.
3. I can't find one pair of matching socks!
4. I shouldn't have waited so long to pack.
5. I haven't checked the dryer yet. I hope they are in there!
6. I would've checked sooner if I wasn't so busy.
7. I've waited too long to find my socks.
8. I don't know what I'm going to do!
9. You'd think I'd own at least one pair of matching socks!
10. It looks like I won't be wearing socks on my trip!

Lesson 12; Exercise 2; Day 57

1. Claire and Ava _____ at church. (present) _____ are
2. Claire and Ava _____ at church. (past) _____ were
3. Claire _____ excited. (past) — is
4. Claire _____ excited. (present) — was
5. I _____ hoping to get a solo in the play. (past) — am
6. I _____ hoping to get a solo in the play. (present) — was

7. AC — Peanut Butter and Jelly
8. PBJ — Air Conditioning
9. Q&A — As Soon As Possible
10. TLC — Question and Answer
11. VIP — Very Important Person
12. ASAP — Tender Loving Care

Lesson 12; Exercise 3; Day 58

State	P.O.	Abbr.
1. Alabama	CA	Calif.
2. Alaska	AR	Ark.
3. Arizona	AL	Ala.
4. Arkansas	AK	
5. California	AZ	Ariz.
6. Colorado	GA	Ga.
7. Connecticut	DE	Del.
8. Delaware	CT	Conn.
9. Florida	CO	Colo.
10. Georgia	FL	Fla.
11. Hawaii	ID	
12. Idaho	IA	
13. Illinois	IN	Ind.
14. Indiana	IL	Ill.
15. Iowa	HI	
16. Kansas	ME	Me.
17. Kentucky	MD	Md.
18. Louisiana	KY	Ky.
19. Maine	LA	La.
20. Maryland	KS	Kan.
21. Massachusetts	MI	Mich.
22. Michigan	MA	Mass.
23. Minnesota	MS	Miss.
24. Mississippi	MO	Mo.
25. Missouri	MN	Minn.

State	P.O.	Abbr.
26. Montana	NJ	N.J.
27. Nebraska	MT	Mont.
28. Nevada	NH	N.H.
29. New Hampshire	NE	Neb.
30. New Jersey	NV	Nev.
31. New Mexico	NC	N.C.
32. New York	ND	N.D.
33. North Carolina	OH	
34. North Dakota	NY	N.Y.
35. Ohio	NM	N.M.
36. Oklahoma	OR	Or.
37. Oregon	OK	Okla.
38. Pennsylvania	PA	Pa.
39. Rhode Island	SC	S.C.
40. South Carolina	RI	R.I.
41. South Dakota	VT	Vt.
42. Tennessee	TX	Tex.
43. Texas	TN	Tenn.
44. Utah	SD	S.D.
45. Vermont	UT	
46. Virginia	WI	Wis.
47. Washington	WV	W. Va.
48. West Virginia	VA	Va.
49. Wisconsin	WY	Wyo.
50. Wyoming	WA	Wash.

Lesson 13; Exercise 2; Day 62

1. I have seen the script of the play.
2. Mrs. Pruitt saw Claire.
3. I see (or saw) Ava and Claire.

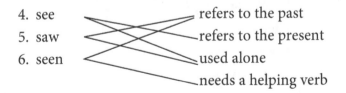

4. see
5. saw
6. seen

refers to the past
refers to the present
used alone
needs a helping verb

7. Jin was really surprised he got a lead part in the play.

8. A real camel would be fun in the play.
9. Claire was really upset she didn't get a lead role in the play.
10. Ava was really sad for Claire.
11. Ava knew she wasn't a real actor.

Lesson 13; Exercise 3; Day 63

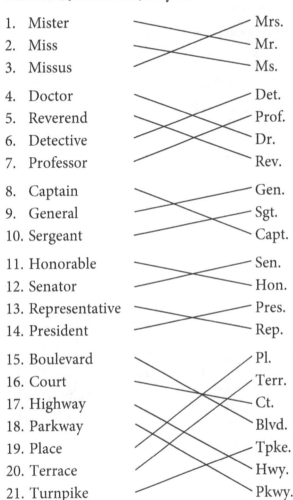

1. Mister
2. Miss
3. Missus
4. Doctor
5. Reverend
6. Detective
7. Professor
8. Captain
9. General
10. Sergeant
11. Honorable
12. Senator
13. Representative
14. President
15. Boulevard
16. Court
17. Highway
18. Parkway
19. Place
20. Terrace
21. Turnpike

Mrs.
Mr.
Ms.
Det.
Prof.
Dr.
Rev.
Gen.
Sgt.
Capt.
Sen.
Hon.
Pres.
Rep.
Pl.
Terr.
Ct.
Blvd.
Tpke.
Hwy.
Pkwy.

1. Illinois
2. Missouri
3. Oklahoma
4. Texas
5. New Mexico
6. Arizona
7. Nevada
8. California
9. Chicago, Los Angeles

Lesson 13; Exercise 5; Day 65

1. leaf = leaves
2. wolf = wolves
3. wife = wives
4. calf = calves
5. life = lives
6. half = halves
7. enemy = enemies
8. country = countries
9. supply = supplies
10. mystery = mysteries
11. twenty = twenties
12. lady = ladies
13. roof = roofs
14. cliff = cliffs

Lesson 14; Exercise 2; Day 67

1. gone
2. go
3. went

present
past
past with helping verb

4. eaten
5. ate
6. eat

present
past
past with helping verb

7. I have __ lunch already.
8. I __ my last peach earlier.
9. I __ peaches every day.

eat
eaten
ate

Lesson 14; Exercise 3; Day 68

Lesson 14; Exercise 5; Day 70

```
X H S O U G B J N E N U F N C
R Q S U O K A O C T O P I K S
E K C W X S R I L N O D H U C
L Q N O N Z M T E Z E T H B C
P U P Y R S G X F E C I P L H
C S X O O N O A W V H K F R O
O O C A C T I A Y S I O P F E
W P E O G F E O A W L I H R Q
B E A N E S I G E G D A P K U
V O N V E E I S A N R L X X X
L P O O S E N S H E E P D N Z
F L L P E E D T O S N B E P B
Y E O Z M C H F R C H L E Y D
A I V O Z U Z I H Y E F R X S
Z K W G K K N A X W M O O S E
```

Lesson 15; Exercise 2; Day 72

1. Singular, far
2. Singular, near
3. Plural, near
4. Plural, far

this
that
these
those

Lesson 15; Exercise 3; Day 73

1. nice: nicer, nicest
2. tall: taller, tallest
3. tasty: tastier, tastiest
4. wet: wetter, wettest
5. great: greater, greatest
6. red: redder, reddest
7. safe: safer, safest
8. happy: happier, happiest

Lesson 15; Exercise 5; Day 75

1. tall taller, tallest
2. great greater, greatest
3. hot hotter, hottest
4. red redder, reddest
5. funny funnier, funniest

6. large larger, largest

7. close closer, closest

Lesson 16; Exercise 1; Day 76

1. cat
2. ball
3. tree
4. run
5. yell
6. jump
7. sweet
8. pretty
9. fast

Lesson 16; Exercise 2; Day 77

1. The camel hid its treat.
2. It's going to be a great play.
3. Who's bringing snacks for play practice?
4. Whose donkey is this?

Lesson 16; Exercise 3; Day 78

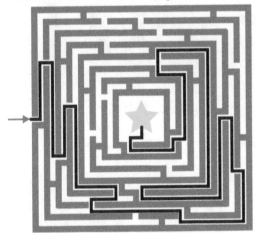

Lesson 16; Exercise 5; Day 80

1. beggar, calendar, collar, polar, sugar
2. answer, chapter, proper, weather
3. director, doctor, labor, motor, sailor

Lesson 17; Exercise 2; Day 82

1. Ava has the most lines in the play.

2. Jin almost knows all of his lines in the play.

3. Micah loves to sit behind the sound board.

4. Claire set the manger on the stage.

Lesson 17; Exercise 3; Day 83

H	L	D	O	N	U	T	A	F	R
A	C	P	A	N	C	A	K	E	Q
M	U	N	K	A	R	C	H	S	A
B	P	S	C	B	L	O	E	A	J
U	C	R	O	I	S	S	A	N	T
R	A	D	Y	B	R	E	A	D	N
G	K	P	A	R	I	S	U	W	C
E	E	Q	H	M	U	F	F	I	N
R	F	P	E	L	M	C	S	C	D
I	C	E	C	R	E	A	M	H	Z

Lesson 17; Exercise 5; Day 85

1. final, metal, pedal, special, total
2. barrel, model, nickel, towel
3. battle, candle, eagle, simple, title

Lesson 18; Exercise 1; Day 86

1. F
2. O
3. O
4. F

Lesson 18; Exercise 2; Day 87

1. Claire and Ava _____ _____ at church. (present) — are

2. Claire and Ava _____ _____ at church. (past) — were

4. Claire _____ excited. (past) — is

5. Claire _____ excited. (present) — was

7. I _____ hoping to get a solo in the play. (past) — am

8. I _____ hoping to get a solo in the play. (present) — was

7. I have **seen** the script of the play.

8. Mrs. Pruitt **saw** Claire.

9. I **see** (or **saw**) Ava and Claire.

10. gone — present
11. go — past
12. went — past with helping verb

13. I have __ lunch already. — eat
14. I __ my last peach earlier. — eaten
15. I __ peaches every day. — ate

16. Singular, far — this
17. Singular, near — that
18. Plural, near — these
19. Plural, far — those

20. The camel hid **its** treat.

21. **It's** going to be a great play.

22. **Who's** bringing snacks for play practice?

23. **Whose** donkey is this?

24. Ava has the **most** lines in the play.

25. Jin knows **almost** all of his lines in the play.

Lesson 18; Exercise 3; Day 88

1. can't — we would
2. she'll — can not
3. they're — she will
4. we'd — they are

5. Answers will vary.
6. Answers will vary.
7. Answers will vary.
8. Mister = **Mr.**
9. Miss = **Ms.**
10. Missus = **Mrs.**
11. Junior = **Jr.**
12. Senior = **Sr.**

13. Boulevard — Tpke.
14. Highway — Blvd.
15. Turnpike — Hwy.

16. Answers will vary.

17. Answers will vary.

18. nice: **nicer, nicest**
19. tall: **taller, tallest**
20. tasty: **tastier, tastiest**
21. wet: **wetter, wettest**

22. figure of speech — does not use the words like or as
23. metaphor — uses the words like or as
24. simile — describes something in a way that is not literal

25. Answers will vary.

A Musical Mystery

1. Piano
2. Xylophone
3. Harp
4. Accordion
5. Castanets (across)
5. Cello (down)
6. Violin
7. Cymbals
8. Synthesizer
9. Triangle
10. Guitar
11. Trumpet
12. Melodica
13. Drum
14. Tambourine
15. Saxophone
16. Maracas

Lesson 19; Exercise 2; Day 92

1. The **small white** <u>dog</u> ran across the **green** <u>grass</u>.
2. The **big red** <u>ball</u> rolled across the **large** <u>lawn</u>.
3. <u>Claire</u> drank the **sour** <u>lemonade</u>.
4. The **noisy** <u>dog</u> barked at the **stinky** <u>skunk</u>.
5. The **two cute** <u>kittens</u> played with the <u>string</u>.
6. The **pokey** <u>porcupine</u> hid behind the <u>tree</u>.

7. The snowy hill made for happy children.
8. The fast sled carried excited boys.

Lesson 19; Exercise 3; Day 93

1. Possible answer: triangle
2. Possible answer: decrease
3. Possible answer: understand
4. Possible answer: misbehave
5. Possible answer: octagon or octopus
6. Possible answer: quadrant
7. Possible answer: nonsense
8. Possible answer: bicycle
9. Possible answer: overheard

Lesson 19; Exercise 5; Day 95

1. nonsense — doesn't make sense; without meaning
2. overheard — heard something without intending to
3. misbehave — did not behave; behaved badly
4. quadrant — of four parts
5. overdone — over cooked; too much
6. bicycle — a vehicle with two wheels
7. misread — read wrongly
8. defeat — conquer
9. octopus — sea creature with eight legs
10. understand — to get the meaning of something
11. decrease — to become smaller or fewer
12. underground — beneath the surface of the ground; in hiding
13. octagon — a shape with eight sides and eight angles
14. triangle — a shape with three sides and three angles

Lesson 20; Exercise 2; Day 97

1. Claire quickly climbed the tree. quickly → climbed
2. The mail came early. early → came
3. Jin happily sang a song. happily → sang

4. Micah never eats pumpkin pie. never → eats

Lesson 20; Exercise 3; Day 98

1. Possible answer: farmer
2. Possible answer: natural
3. Possible answer: colonial
4. Possible answer: conductor
5. Possible answer: vacation
6. Possible answer: illness
7. Possible answer: wooden
8. Possible answer: enjoyment

Lesson 20; Exercise 5; Day 100

1. kindness — a kind act
2. builder — a person who constructs something
3. partial — in part
4. farmer — a person who manages a farm
5. wooden — made of wood
6. colonial — living in colonies
7. actor — a person who acts on a stage, in movies, or on TV
8. illness — a disease or sickness
9. conductor — a person who directs or is in charge
10. enjoyment — taking pleasure in something
11. natural — existing in nature
12. dental — of or for the teeth
13. vacation — a time away for recreation or travel
14. creation — the act of creating

Lesson 21; Exercise 1; Day 101

1. green route
2. pink route
3. orange route
4. pink route

Lesson 21; Exercise 2; Day 102

1. The squirrel ran into the tree.
   preposition = into; OP = tree

2. Micah jumped <u>on the trampoline</u>. preposition = on; OP = trampoline

3. Jin played <u>with Micah</u>. preposition = with; OP = Micah

4. The boys went <u>inside the house</u>. preposition = inside; OP = house

Lesson 21; Exercise 3; Day 103

1. understandable: prefix-under suffix-able root word-stand

2. distrusted: prefix-dis suffix-ed root word-trust

3. Possible answer: disrupt or erupt

4. Possible answer: terrain or territory

5. Possible answer: geology or geography

6. Possible answer: photocopy or photograph

7. Possible answer: subtract or traction

8. Possible answer: odometer or perimeter

9. Possible answer: metric or metronome

Lesson 21; Exercise 5; Day 105

1. erupt — explode with fire and noise

2. metric — based on the meter

3. terrain — a stretch of land

4. geography — the study of the earth's surface features and people

5. disrupt — to break up or cause a disturbance

6. subtract — take away

7. territory — land belonging to a government or ruler

8. geology — science dealing with the composition of the earth

9. photograph — a picture made using a camera

10. traction — grip, pulling of something over a surface such as a road

11. perimeter — the boundary of an area or object

12. metronome — a device that marks time

13. photocopy — a duplicate copy of something printed or written

14. odometer — an instrument that measures the distance traveled

Lesson 22; Exercise 2; Day 107

1. homophones
2. homonyms

- sound the same
- different meanings
- spelled the same
- spelled different

Lesson 22; Exercise 5; Day 110

1. pray, prey

2. pane, pain

3. sale, sail

4. blew, blue

5. dear, deer

6. beat, beet

7. wait, weight

Lesson 23; Exercise 5; Day 115

1. bark

2. bear

3. change

4. fire

5. foot

6. handle

7. iron

8. left

9. organ

10. pound

11. rock

12. rose

13. squash

14. trunk

Lesson 24; Exercise 2; Day 117

1. The wind blew Jin's ball across the yard.

2. Micah must wind the toy dog for it to walk.

3. different meanings

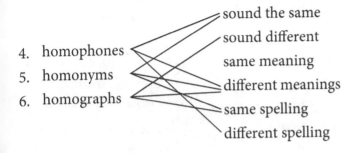

4. homophones
5. homonyms
6. homographs

sound the same
sound different
same meaning
different meanings
same spelling
different spelling

Lesson 24; Exercise 3; Day 118

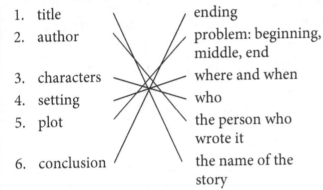

1. title
2. author
3. characters
4. setting
5. plot
6. conclusion

ending
problem: beginning, middle, end
where and when
who
the person who wrote it
the name of the story

Lesson 24; Exercise 5; Day 120

```
X  S  W  R  W  A  I  N  C  L  U  D  E  A  C
P  W  B  H  S  P  K  M  E  G  T  J  M  U  J
H  T  L  E  O  J  B  C  T  C  V  B  T  A  K
Z  N  F  G  Y  M  N  A  S  T  I  C  S  T  Y
U  P  I  H  A  I  T  I  S  P  H  N  O  U  Z
Y  U  V  Z  S  D  O  G  B  C  L  R  M  E  L
F  P  K  M  B  A  T  R  M  R  R  B  C  P  T
P  S  X  X  H  V  J  A  Q  A  J  Y  O  J  Z
W  Y  O  G  U  R  T  N  C  F  A  Y  U  R  Y
N  E  G  A  B  C  I  T  I  Z  E  N  N  X  I
X  D  I  T  O  J  I  E  I  H  H  Y  T  M  A
G  G  N  H  U  E  T  D  G  V  R  R  R  B  M
R  E  G  E  N  F  Z  L  W  I  A  T  Y  G  R
M  S  E  R  C  Y  M  B  A  L  S  M  V  V  I
I  T  R  Q  E  T  J  B  R  D  A  M  A  G  E
```

Lesson 25; Exercise 1; Day 121

1. Fact
2. The Bible tells us this happened.

Lesson 26; Exercise 5; Day 130

1. afternoon
2. alphabet
3. behavior
4. compromise
5. direction
6. document
7. edible
8. family
9. following
10. holiday
11. internet
12. navigate
13. remember
14. suddenly

Lesson 27; Exercise 2; Day 132

1. Answers will vary.
2. a
3. an
4. the

used before words that start with a vowel
used to refer to a specific noun
used before words that start with a consonant

5. Answers will vary.
6. The squirrel ran into the tree. preposition = into, OP = tree
7. The boys went inside the house. preposition = inside, OP = house
8. Answers will vary.

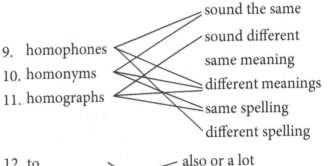

9. homophones
10. homonyms
11. homographs

sound the same
sound different
same meaning
different meanings
same spelling
different spelling

12. to
13. too
14. two

also or a lot
a number
direction

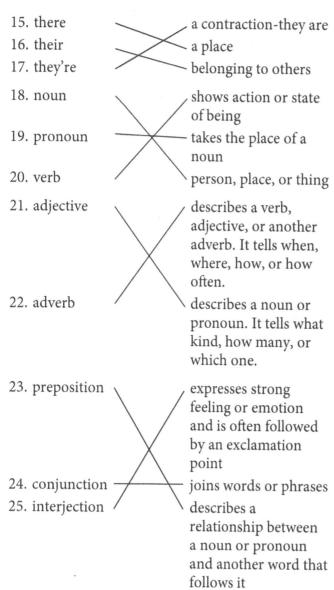

15. there — a place
16. their — belonging to others
17. they're — a contraction-they are
18. noun — person, place, or thing
19. pronoun — takes the place of a noun
20. verb — shows action or state of being
21. adjective — describes a noun or pronoun. It tells what kind, how many, or which one.
22. adverb — describes a verb, adjective, or another adverb. It tells when, where, how, or how often.
23. preposition — describes a relationship between a noun or pronoun and another word that follows it
24. conjunction — joins words or phrases
25. interjection — expresses strong feeling or emotion and is often followed by an exclamation point

Lesson 27; Exercise 3; Day 133

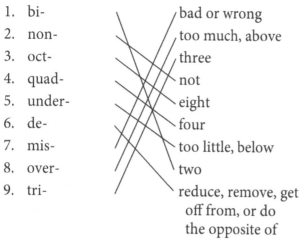

1. bi- — two
2. non- — not
3. oct- — eight
4. quad- — four
5. under- — too little, below
6. de- — reduce, remove, get off from, or do the opposite of
7. mis- — bad or wrong
8. over- — too much, above
9. tri- — three

10. -al — related to, character of
11. -en — become, made of, resemble, to make
12. -er — one who, that which
13. -ial — related to, character of
14. -ness — condition, state of
15. -ment — act, result, or state of
16. -or — one who, that which
17. -tion — act, process

18. rupt — break or burst
19. terr — land
20. geo — earth, ground, or soil
21. photo — light
22. tract — pull or drag
23. meter or metr — measure

24. It is where and when the story takes place.

25. It is what happens in the story. It tells us what the conflict or the problem is, what happens, and how the conflict or problem is solved. It has a beginning, middle, and end.

Bonus: Answers will vary.

Lesson 28; Exercise 2; Day 137

1. tree: trees'
2. dog: dogs'
3. Micah and Jin
4.

B	Q	J	I	J	S	W	B
D	B	T	W	B	I	R	D
O	I	E	A	U	D	J	I
J	R	D	I	R	D	Y	D
I	N	F	B	K	B	T	R
U	M	D	J	O	I	D	I
B	I	R	Y	H	R	L	B
G	Q	V	J	B	D	E	I

Lesson 28; Exercise 3; Day 138

1. Imperative — gives a command
2. Declarative — makes a statement
3. Exclamatory — expresses strong emotion
4. Interrogative — asks a question

5. Imperative .
6. Declarative .
7. Exclamatory !
8. Interrogative ?
9. Did Claire make the flashcards, Micah?
10. Micah washed the dishes, folded his clothes, and made his bed.
11. Ava, did you eat popcorn?
12. How long, Jin, did it take to memorize the books of the Bible?
13. Possible answer:

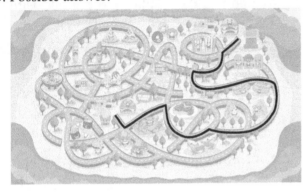

Lesson 28; Exercise 5; Day 140

1. belong
2. blanket
3. bling
4. drink
5. frequent
6. least
7. saint
8. scared
9. scope
10. skirt
11. skunk
12. starve
13. swept
14. tempt

Lesson 29; Exercise 2; Day 142

1. waltz = waltzes
2. rock = rocks
3. box = boxes
4. hero = heroes
5. bush = bushes
6. photo = photos
7. chimney = chimneys
8. church = churches
9. radio = radios
10. fuss = fusses
11. calf = calves
12. mystery = mysteries

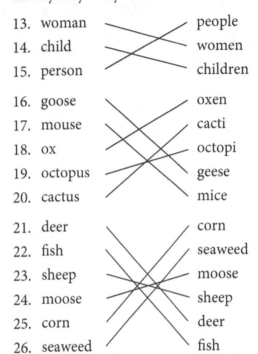

13. woman — people
14. child — women
15. person — children

16. goose — oxen
17. mouse — cacti
18. ox — octopi
19. octopus — geese
20. cactus — mice

21. deer — corn
22. fish — seaweed
23. sheep — moose
24. moose — sheep
25. corn — deer
26. seaweed — fish

Lesson 29; Exercise 3; Day 143

1. Micah was nervous about his new class?
2. Dad said Micah would learn a life lesson.
3. Alexia wanted
4. micah might make some new friends.
5. He had a lot on his mind!
6. Micah wanted Jin in his class.
7. Micah was the youngest in his class.
8. Micah and Claire went to their class.
9. fanboys
10. You can either go swimming or weed the garden.
11. I like spring, but I love fall.
12. It is snowing heavily, so I can go sledding.

13. I like apples, but I love peaches.

14.

```
A D I N I N G R R A
T R A L L E C O A G
T I C N K I P O G E
L A U U Y T O M L I
M Y N R R C R C H V
O A D S E H E N H I
O R R A S E N G A N
R D Y B B M E A L G
H T A B E E D R L R
M O O R D N T M O O
```

Lesson 30; Exercise 2; Day 147

1. Micah went <u>into his room</u>. preposition = into, OP = room

2. Claire studied <u>during lunch</u>. preposition = during, OP = lunch

3. on

4. between

5. behind

6. beside

7. in

8. under

9. above

10. before

11. near

12. in

13. on

14. over

15. in

16. in

17. behind

18. near

Lesson 30; Exercise 3; Day 148

1. "I better get back to my class," said Jin as he slowly left the room.

2. Claire asked, "Micah, did you show Jin the Temple?"

Lesson 30; Exercise 5; Day 150

1. I hurt my ankle. I have a sprain.

2. I cough to clear my throat.

3. I shrug when I lift my shoulders up and down.

4. The little shrimp are cute swimming in the ocean.

5. I don't like to scrape my knee when I fall.

6. I sew with a needle and thread.

7. Would you like to split a piece of cake with me?

8. A shape with four equal sides and four corners is called a square.

9. I am careful when I squat down not to strain my back.

10. I see a sprout coming from the seed I planted.

11. Sometimes I like to splurge and buy a large ice cream cone.

12. We had to strip the old paint off the wall before we could paint.

13. I like to scramble my eggs before I cook them.

Lesson 31; Exercise 2; Day 152

1. bi-   bad or wrong
2. non-   too much, above
3. oct-   three
4. quad-   not
5. under-   eight
6. de-   four
7. mis-   too little, below
8. over-   two
9. tri-   reduce, remove, get off from, or do the opposite of

10. -al

11. -en

12. -er

13. -ial

14. -ness

15. -ment

16. -or

17. -tion

act, result, or state of

act, process

related to, character of

become, made of, resemble, to make

one who, that which

condition, state of

18. rupt

19. terr

20. geo

21. photo

22. tract

23. meter or metr

earth, ground, or soil

break or burst

measure

land

light

pull or drag

Lesson 31; Exercise 3; Day 153

1. Answers will vary.

2. Answers will vary.

3. Answers will vary.

4. Mister = Mr.

5. Miss = Ms.

6. Missus = Mrs.

7. Junior = Jr.

8. Senior = Sr.

9. Boulevard

10. Highway

11. Turnpike

Tpke.

Blvd.

Hwy.

Lesson 31; Exercise 5; Day 155

1. enough, laugh, rough

2. elephant, gopher, graph, nephew, phone, phrase, physical

3. awful, forever, fossil, freedom

Lesson 32; Exercise 1; Day 156

1. Red

2. Orange

3. Yellow

4. Blue

5. Three

Lesson 32; Exercise 2; Day 157

1. H

2. L

3. H

4. L

Lesson 32; Exercise 3; Day 158

1. Tap 1 = B

2. Tap 2 = D

3. Tap 3 = A

4. Tap 4 = C

5. Tap 5 = E

Lesson 32; Exercise 5; Day 160

1. nickel, pocket, snack

2. kangaroo, kayak, napkin

3. anchor, chorus

4. circus, create, curious

5. quality, quiet, squid

Lesson 33; Exercise 2; Day 162

1. future

2. past

3. present

4. could be eating

5. They _____ at church. _____ are
(present)

6. They _____ at church. _____ were
(past)

Lesson 33; Exercise 3; Day 163

1. sail = sāl

2. ship = shĭp

Lesson 33; Exercise 5; Day 165

```
X N M Q Z L I I A O J H Y M N
F Q X D F G I F Q H S Z S H M
F H M G E A M S P L V H R Y V
R C A L F M J F T E H C H G C
D K G R H U K W J E O P R M A
U N I P L U M B E R N E L V M
L I V W P U G G E P O H T G Q
M F F H H J C W E Q R Z H P B
G E L E L U S K N I G H T M I
N L O E W N K J C J E P U D K
A O W Z A E U N X X K H R D W
W F D E S I G N Z C T P R P S
B E P I W R E N C H B O Y H V
H Y F K P T L Q V Q W U N A I
R A M F K L N W T S X W M F P
```

Lesson 34; Exercise 1; Day 166

1. Student should name a sport.
2. Student should name a farm animal.
3. Student should name something that is worn on feet.
4. Student should name something that lives in the ocean.

Lesson 34; Exercise 2; Day 167

1. quickly → climbed
2. never → eats

Lesson 34; Exercise 3; Day 168

1. conclusion —————— ending
2. author   problem: beginning, middle, end
3. characters   where and when
4. setting   who
5. plot   the person who wrote it

Lesson 34; Exercise 5; Day 170

1. cattle
2. collar

3. essay
4. giggle
5. mirror
6. mitten
7. pepper
8. rabbit
9. riddle
10. shuffle
11. squirrel
12. suffer
13. tunnel
14. valley

Lesson 35; Exercise 2; Day 172

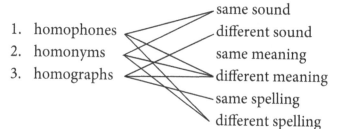

1. homophones
2. homonyms
3. homographs

same sound
different sound
same meaning
different meaning
same spelling
different spelling

Lesson 35; Exercise 5; Day 175

1. 11 = eleventh
2. 12 = twelfth
3. 13 = thirteenth
4. 14 = fourteenth
5. 15 = fifteenth
6. 16 = sixteenth
7. 17 = seventeenth
8. 18 = eighteenth
9. 19 = nineteenth
10. 20 = twentieth
11. 21 = twenty-first
12. 22 = twenty-second
13. 23 = twenty-third
14. 24 = twenty-fourth

Lesson 36; Exercise 2; Day 177

1. Possible answer: Christmas or Easter

2. mom = mom's
3. moms = moms'
4. chimney = chimneys
5. church = churches
6. radio = radios
7. half = halves
8. bakery = bakeries

9. goose — oxen
10. mouse — mice
11. ox — geese

12. Micah went <u>into his room</u>. preposition = into, OP = room
13. Answers will vary.

14. quad- — one who, that which
15. -al or -ial — four
16. -er or -or — earth, ground, or soil
17. geo — related to, character of

18. H
19. L
20. Answers will vary.
21. Answers will vary.
22. Answers will vary.

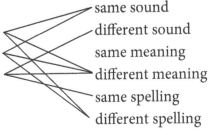

23. homophones — same sound
24. homonyms — different sound
25. homographs — same meaning
  different meaning
  same spelling
  different spelling

Lost Letters

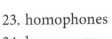

```
B O N D E N V E L O P E
C P Y P B W E D C H S M
P O S T O F F I C E A L
Y S E P X E H D N E U F
F T H N O N E H O N C W
P M P A C H P A R C E L
G A M R N O O U W O V I
O N R A F H S T U F W G
L E T T E R T T H B Z N
F U E H O M B C A H I D
C O K N D O O E C M U X
K B O F C I X R S H P J
```

Lesson 36; Exercise 3; Day 178

1. IN Why did the students make flashcards?
2. D I like to memorize the books of the Bible.
3. E God is good!
4. IM Get out your Bible.
5. Did Claire make the flashcards, Micah?
6. Micah washed the dishes, folded his clothes, and made his bed.
7. Ava, did you eat popcorn?
8. How long, Jin, did it take to memorize the books of the Bible?
9. Answers will vary.
10. <u>Micah</u> wanted Jin in his class.
11. Possible answer: I like apples, but I love peaches.
12. Answers will vary.

13. Boulevard — Blvd.
14. Highway — Tpke.
15. Turnpike — Hwy.

16. Answers will vary.
17. Answers will vary.
18. Answers will vary.
19. Answers will vary.
20. Answers will vary.

21. conclusion — ending
22. author — problem: beginning, middle, end
23. characters — where and when
24. setting — who
25. plot — the person who wrote it